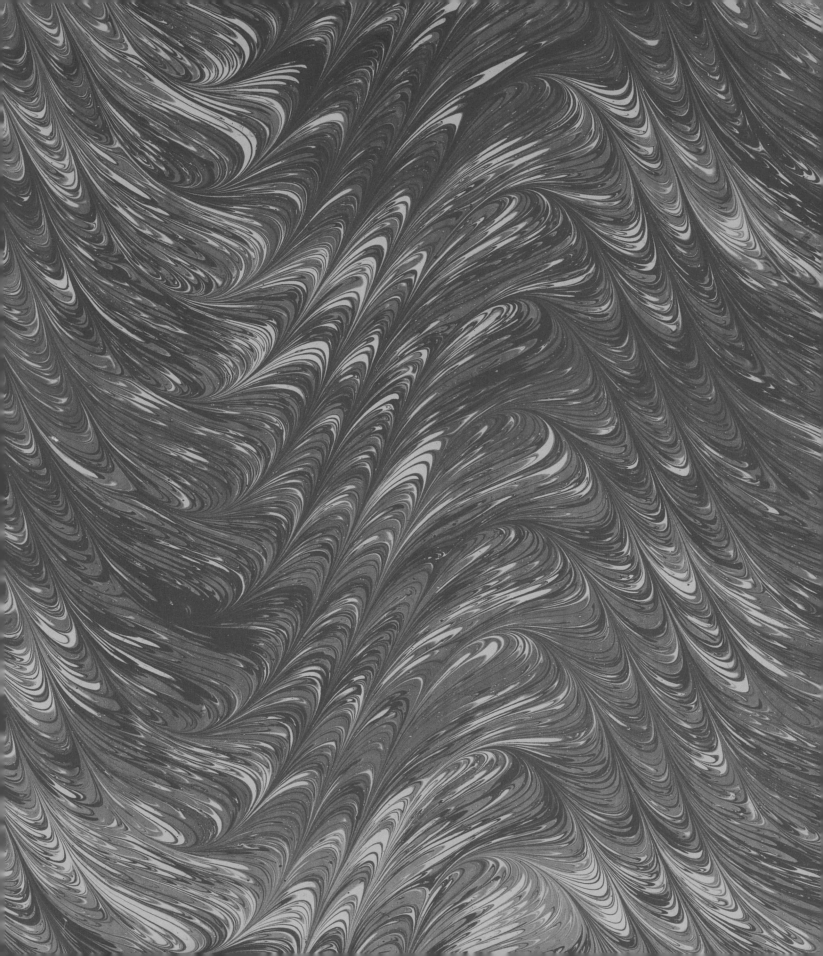

HARCOURT

· TROPHIES ·

A HARCOURT READING/LANGUAGE ARTS PROGRAM

JUST FOR YOU

SENIOR AUTHORS
Isabel L. Beck ◆ Roger C. Farr ◆ Dorothy S. Strickland

AUTHORS
Alma Flor Ada ◆ Marcia Brechtel ◆ Margaret McKeown
Nancy Roser ◆ Hallie Kay Yopp

SENIOR CONSULTANT
Asa G. Hilliard III

CONSULTANTS
F. Isabel Campoy ◆ David A. Monti

Harcourt

Orlando   Boston   Dallas   Chicago   San Diego

Visit *The Learning Site!*

www.harcourtschool.com

Dear Reader,

We have chosen these stories and selections *just for you!* In **Just For You,** you will read about characters whose differences make them special. You will find out how helping others can be fun and can make you feel good about yourself. You will learn how many different things in nature grow and change.

We hope you will like each selection.

Sincerely,

The Authors

The Authors

Being Me

CONTENTS

Reading
**Across
Texts**

Helping Hands

CONTENTS

Reading
Across
Texts

Reading
Across
Texts

Our World

CONTENTS

9

Using Reading Strategies

A strategy is a plan for doing something well.
You can use strategies when you read to help you understand a story better. First, **look at the title and pictures.** Then, **think about what you want to find out.** Using strategies like these can help you become a better reader.

Look at the list of strategies on page 11. You will learn how to use these strategies as you read the stories in this book. As you read, look back at the list to remind yourself of the **strategies good readers use.**

- Use Decoding/ Phonics
- Look at Word Bits and Parts
- Self-Correct
- Read Ahead
- Reread Aloud

- Make and Confirm Predictions
- Sequence Events/Summarize
- Create Mental Images
- Use Context to Confirm Meaning
- Make Inferences

Here are some ways to make sure you understand what you are reading:

✔ Copy the list of strategies onto a piece of construction paper.

✔ Fold it and use it as a bookmark as you read.

✔ After you read, talk with a classmate about the strategies you used.

Being Me

CONTENTS

Vocabulary Power

dull

exciting

handsome

hardly

sideways

sparkling

spotted

Last week my class took a field trip to a wild animal park. It was so **exciting**! I could **hardly** wait to see the big cats.

First I **spotted** a leopard taking a nap. She looked warm and cuddly.

14

Then I saw a lion with a great mane of hair. He turned his head **sideways** and roared.

Finally I saw a **handsome** tiger with thick, striped fur. He lay by a pool of water that was **sparkling** in the sunlight. When he turned and looked at me, I shivered!

I think the big cats are the most interesting animals in the park. They are never **dull**!

Vocabulary-Writing CONNECTION

Write about an **exciting** place that you would like to visit. Tell why you want to go there.

Award-Winning
Author/Illustrator

Genre

Fantasy

A fantasy is a story that takes place in a make-believe world.

Look for

- story events that could not happen in real life.

- characters that may be make-believe.

16

The Mixed-Up Chameleon

by Eric Carle

On a shiny green leaf sat a small green chameleon.
It moved onto a brown tree and turned brownish.
Then it rested on a red flower and turned reddish.
When the chameleon moved slowly across the yellow
sand, it turned yellowish. You could hardly see it.

When the chameleon
was warm and had
something to eat, it
turned sparkling green.

But when it was cold and hungry,
it turned gray and dull.

20

When the chameleon was hungry,
it sat still and waited.
Only its eyes moved—up, down, sideways—
until it spotted a fly.
Then the chameleon's long and sticky tongue
shot out and caught the fly.
That was its life.
It was not very exciting.
But one day...

... the chameleon saw a zoo!
It had never seen so many beautiful animals.

ZOO

23

The chameleon thought:

How small I am, how slow, how weak!
I wish I could be big and white like a polar bear.
And the chameleon's wish came true.
But was it happy?
No!

24

25

I wish I could be handsome like a flamingo.

26

I wish I could be smart like a fox.

28

I wish I could swim like a fish.

30

I wish I could run like a deer.

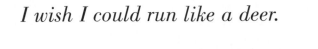

32

33

I wish I could see things far away like a giraffe.

35

I wish I could hide in a shell like a turtle.

36

I wish I could be strong like an elephant.

38

39

I wish I could be funny like a seal.

40

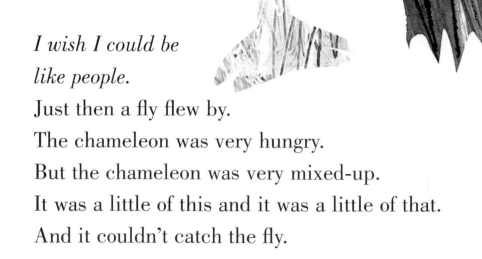

*I wish I could be
like people.*
Just then a fly flew by.
The chameleon was very hungry.
But the chameleon was very mixed-up.
It was a little of this and it was a little of that.
And it couldn't catch the fly.

42

43

I wish I could be myself.
The chameleon's wish came true.
And it caught the fly!

Think and Respond

1. What happened after the chameleon **spotted** the zoo?
2. Why did Eric Carle title his book *The Mixed-Up Chameleon*?
3. What does it mean to "be yourself"?
4. Have you felt the way the mixed-up chameleon feels? Why?
5. Which strategies helped you read this story?

Meet the Author and Illustrator

Dear Readers,

I got the idea for *The Mixed-Up Chameleon* by talking to children just like you. When I visited schools, I asked children to tell me their favorite animals. On a large sheet of paper, I drew the most important part of each animal, such as a fox's tail, an elephant's trunk, and a giraffe's neck. These pictures gave me the idea for this story. I hope you had fun reading it.

Best wishes,

 Visit *The Learning Site!* www.harcourtschool.com

Fun Animal Facts: Cham

To hide from its enemies, a chameleon changes colors. If you could do that, you'd never need new clothes!

eleons

Chameleons have tongues that are longer than their bodies. They whip them out to zap their food!

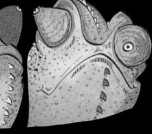

A chameleon can move one of its eyes without moving the other. All the better to see you with, my dear!

Think and Respond

How is the chameleon a special animal?

Making Connections

Compare Texts

1 Why do you think this story is in a theme called Being Me?

2 The chameleon changes many times, but he is still not happy. Why? Tell how you know.

3 "The Mixed-Up Chameleon" is make-believe. "Fun Animal Facts" gives facts. Which one would you read if you wanted to find out what chameleons are really like? Why?

A Special Animal

The chameleon thinks each zoo animal is special. Use a web like this one to brainstorm ideas about an animal you think is special. Then write a sentence about your animal.

Writing CONNECTION

Why a bear is special

How Animals Hide

A chameleon can change colors to hide. Find out the different ways that other animals hide. Then make a "How Animals Hide" mobile with a clothes hanger, string, and index cards. On each card, show an animal and write what it does to hide.

Turtles hide in their shells.

BAby seals have white fur to help them hide in the snow.

People We Admire

The chameleon wanted to be more like other animals. Think about someone you want to be like. Give a short talk for classmates. Name the person you want to be like, and explain why. Speak clearly so your classmates can understand you.

I want to be like Sally Ride because she was brave when she went into space!

51

Main Idea

The most important idea of a paragraph or story is the **main idea**. Other sentences tell about the main idea.

Read the following paragraph.

Mel and her mom made a tasty soup with many things in it. Mel did not know if she wanted noodles or rice, so she added both. Mel did not know if she wanted carrots or celery, so she added both. Mel did not know if she wanted potatoes or beans. Again, she added both. They called it mixed-up soup.

To find the main idea, think about what the story is mostly about.

Test Prep

Main Idea

Read the paragraph. Then answer the questions.

A Special Day

Marcos will be eight on Tuesday. He will have a party at school. His mom will make his favorite foods for dinner. His sister will give him a present. She has brown hair. Marcos can not wait until Tuesday.

1. **What is the main idea of the paragraph?**

   ○ Marcos will eat his favorite foods.

   ○ Marcos will get a present.

   ○ Marcos will have a birthday on Tuesday.

   ○ Marcos will be happy.

Tip

Think about the sentence that tells what the paragraph is mostly about.

2. **Which sentence does not belong in the paragraph?**

   ○ Marcos will be eight on Tuesday.

   ○ His mom will make his favorite foods for dinner.

   ○ His sister will give him a present.

   ○ She has brown hair.

Vocabulary Power

▲ Get Up and Go!

- always
- homework
- minutes
- snuggle
- treat

Every day when I get home from school, I **always** have a special snack. Today my **treat** is an apple with peanut butter.

I always study and do my **homework** before I go outside to play.

54

It takes me a half hour, or 30 **minutes** to finish my homework. Once it's done, I can play until dinnertime.

After dinner, I like to read. I sit on the couch in the living room. My cat, Barney, likes to **snuggle** with me then.

Vocabulary-Writing CONNECTION

Write a few sentences about when and how you do your **homework** each day.

55

Genre

Informational Book

An informational book gives facts about a topic.

Look for

- **a story that gives information.**

- **pictures that help you understand the topic.**

Get Up

and Go!

by
Stuart J. Murphy

illustrated by
Diane Greenseid

You're always so slow.
Let's get up and go!

*Just 5 minutes more
to snuggle with Teddy.*

If you don't get up
you'll never be ready.

A 3-minute stop—
that's all I'll take.

I'd better see how much
time that will make.

She's already late—so I'd better try
to keep careful track of the time going by.

I can show her 5-minute snuggle with Teddy like this.

3 minutes to wash looks like this.

Now I'll put my lines together.

How many minutes have gone by so far?

Then 8 minutes to eat—
I like breakfast the most.

I only wish that you'd
toss me some toast.

Now 2 minutes extra
to give Sammie a treat.

Dog snacks are great.
I'm ready to eat.

She's going upstairs and still has a lot to do.
I'd better keep track of these minutes, too.

I'll show the 8 minutes she took to eat breakfast.

Then 2 minutes to give me a treat looks like this.

I'll put these lines together. How many minutes
have gone by?

Now I'll add this line to my first line.

How many minutes have gone by now?

Then 6 minutes to brush—
both my teeth and my hair.

You're still running late,
but I'm sure you don't care.

And 7 to dress.
That's all I need.

Unless you play games . . .
or sit down to read.

She's taking so long. I'm never sure why.
I'd better check how much time has gone by.

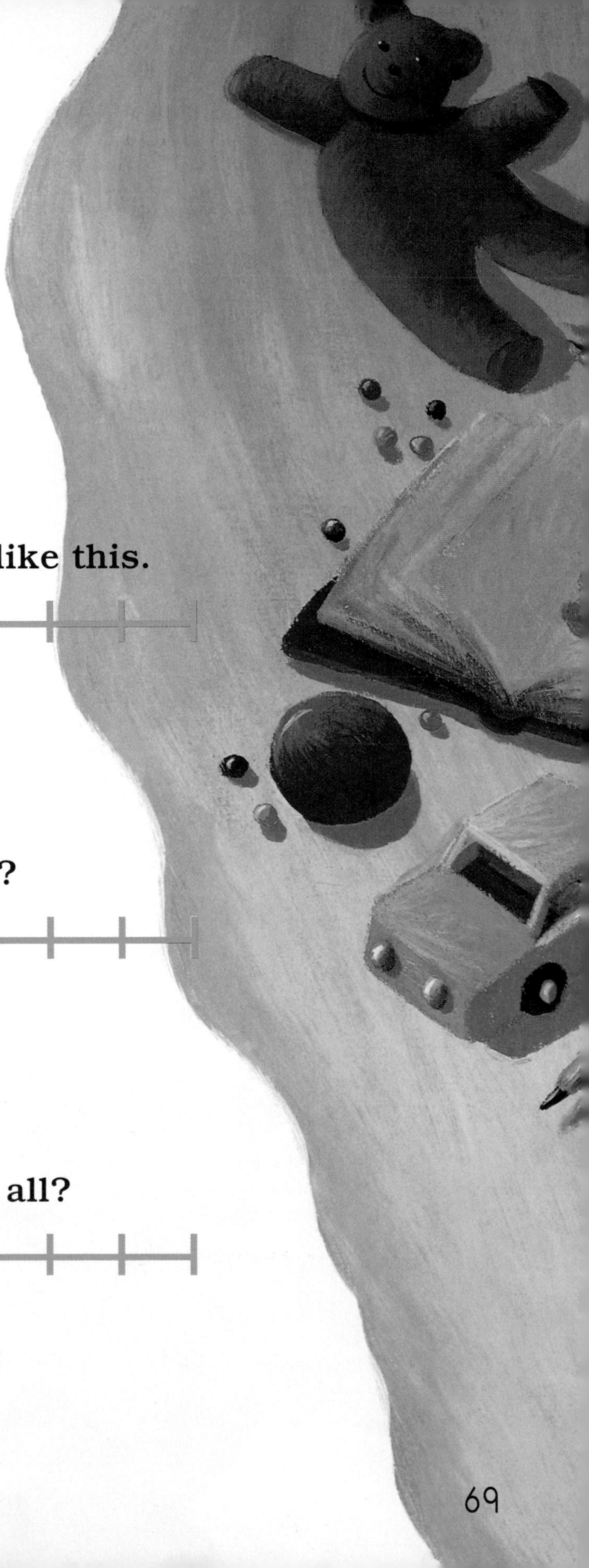

6 minutes to brush looks like this.

And I can show 7 minutes to dress like this.

Now I'll put them together.
How many minutes do we have now?

Then I'll put all my lines together.
How many minutes have gone by in all?

69

Now 4 minutes to pack
all the things I can find.

Make sure that you don't
leave your homework behind!

*A 1-minute hug
and I'll be out the door.*

I wish you had time
for just one hug more.

She's finally on her way—she was almost too late.
Now that she's off, everything will be great.

I'll show 4 minutes to pack.

Then I'll show my 1-minute hug.

If I put them together, they'll look like this.
How many minutes do we have now?

Next I'll put all the lines together.
Now how many minutes have gone by in all?

Now I know how much time she took to get ready,
from the time she woke up and snuggled with Teddy.

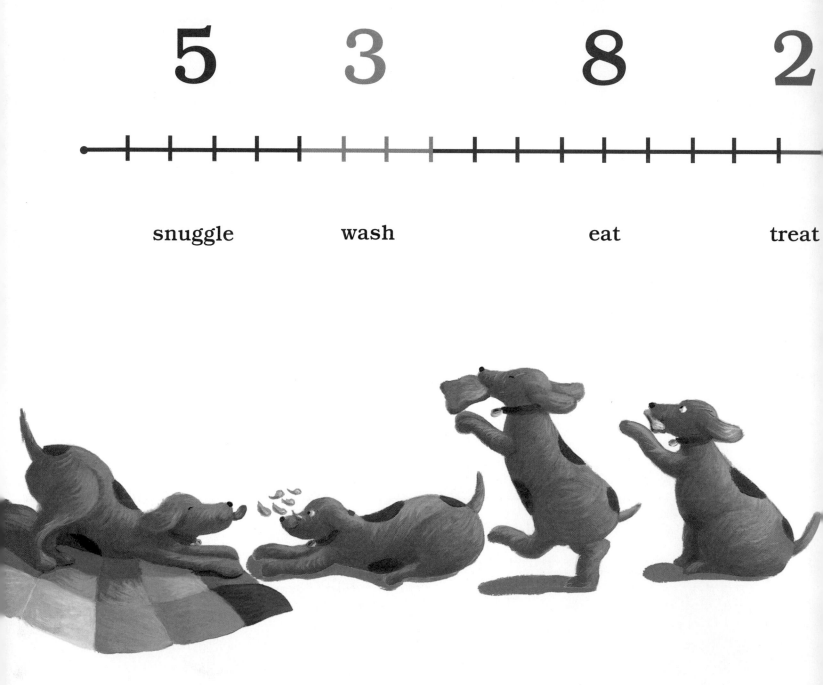

5   3   8   2

snuggle   wash   eat   treat

She took 5 and 3, 8 and 2, 6 and 7, 4 and 1.
That's 36 minutes—and my work was done!

6   7   4   1

brush   dress   pack   hug

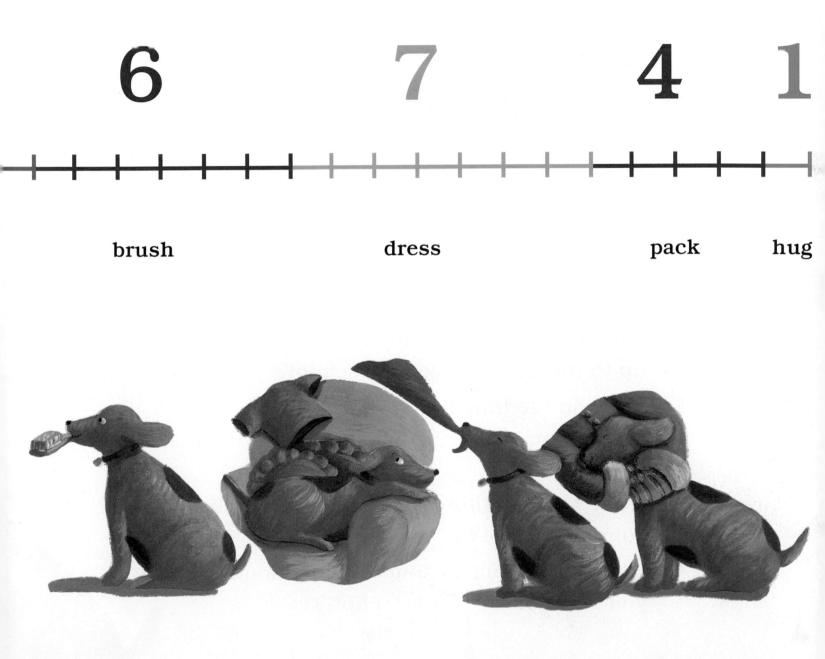

Now she's off to school, and I'm feeling fine.
The rest of the day is totally mine!

Think and Respond

1 What does the girl do from the time she wakes up to the time she goes to school?

2 What do the time lines show?

3 Why do you think the author uses words that rhyme?

4 What kinds of things do you **always** do before going to school?

5 How did reading sentences again aloud help you understand this selection?

Meet the Author and Illustrator

Stuart J. Murphy loves to write children's books about math. He wants to show that people use math every day, even when they are getting ready for school. Like Sammie in the story, his dog, Blitzen, gets him up every morning.

Diane Greenseid has two dogs named Ida and Rosie. They always make sure that she is up for breakfast—*their* breakfast!

Visit *The Learning Site!*
www.harcourtschool.com

Making Connections

Compare Texts

1 Why do you think "Get Up and Go!" is in a theme called Being Me?

2 Do you think the authors of "Get Up and Go!" and "The Mixed-Up Chameleon" had the same or different reasons for writing? Explain.

3 Tell about the setting in this story. Is the girl's home like homes you know? Explain.

Good Dog!

Write notes in a chart to compare the dog in the story to dogs you know about. How is the dog in this story the same as dogs you know or have read about? How is he different?

Writing CONNECTION

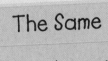

The Same	Different
• wakes girl up in the morning	• can tell time
•	•
•	•

How Many Minutes?

How many minutes will it take for you to get ready for school? Make a prediction. Then time yourself one day. Write down the time you wake up. Then get ready for school. Write down the time you finish. Subtract your start time from your end time to find out how long it took you to get ready. Was your prediction correct?

What Do You Do First?

Watch how the adults in your home get ready for their day. Do you do things in the same order? Make a chart like this one to compare the order in which you and an adult do things. Fill in the chart with what you observe.

	Grandfather	Me
Wash up	1	3
Eat	3	1
Brush teeth	4	2
Get dressed	2	4
Say good-bye	5	5

79

Words with
ame and *ake*

Read these words from "Get Up and Go!"

take   **make**

What is the same about both words? They have the same word part, **ake**.

Now read the next words.

games   **fame**

Do you see the word part **ame** in both words?

You can make new words that end with *ake* and *ame*. Blend the letters below with a word part. How many new words can you make?

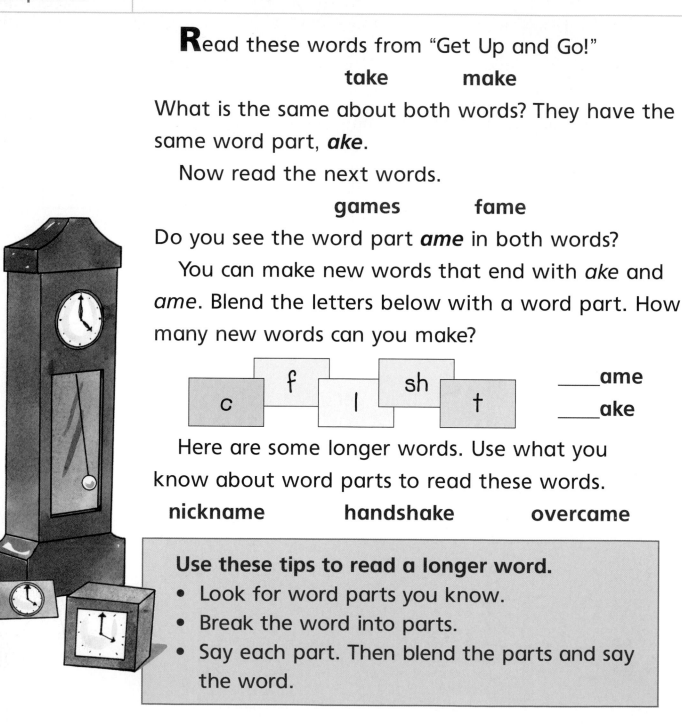

c   f   l   sh   t   ____ame   ____ake

Here are some longer words. Use what you know about word parts to read these words.

nickname   **handshake**   **overcame**

Use these tips to read a longer word.
- Look for word parts you know.
- Break the word into parts.
- Say each part. Then blend the parts and say the word.

80

Test Prep

Words with _ame_ and _ake_

Find the word that has the same sound as the underlined letters in the first word.

Example: **b<u>ake</u>**
- ○ name
- ○ bike
- ● lake

1.   **sh<u>ame</u>**
- ○ sham
- ○ cake
- ○ blame

2.   **snowfl<u>ake</u>**
- ○ black
- ○ mistake
- ○ stack

3.   **<u>came</u>**
- ○ same
- ○ bloom
- ○ Maine

Tip
Look at the underlined letters closely. Be sure you know the sound they make.

Tip
Skip any choices that don't make sense.

81

▲ Henry and Mudge
Under the
Yellow Moon

chipmunks

picked

sniffing

south

woods

Vocabulary Power

Last week my class took a trip to a state park. We walked around in the **woods** all day.

A park ranger greeted us. "You are lucky to be here today," she said. "Many Canada geese have stopped for a rest. They are on their way **south** for the winter."

82

The park ranger warned us not to touch the plants. "Last week, a visitor **picked** a plant from the woods. He didn't know it was poison ivy. He got a bad rash."

Then we went for a nature walk. We saw **chipmunks**, rabbits, birds, and even a deer **sniffing** at berries on a tree. It was exciting to see the animals up close.

Vocabulary–Writing CONNECTION

Imagine that you are taking a nature walk in the **woods**. Write about the plants and animals you see.

HENRY AND MUDGE
UNDER THE
Yellow Moon
Story by Cynthia Rylant
Pictures by Suçie Stevenson

Genre

Realistic Fiction

Realistic fiction is a story with events like those in real life.

Look for

- **a setting that could be a real place.**

- **characters that do things real people do.**

84

Henry
Under

and **Mudge**
the Yellow Moon

Story by Cynthia Rylant
Pictures by Suçie Stevenson

Together in the Fall

In the fall,
Henry and his big dog Mudge
took long walks in the woods.

Henry loved looking at
the tops of the trees.
He liked the leaves:
orange, yellow, brown, and red.

Mudge loved sniffing at the ground.

And he liked the leaves, too.

He always ate a few.

In the fall,
Henry liked counting the birds
flying south.
Mudge liked
watching for busy chipmunks.

Since one was a boy
and the other was a dog,
they never did things
just the same way.

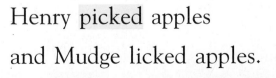

Henry picked apples
and Mudge licked apples.

Henry put on a coat
and Mudge grew one.
And when the fall wind blew,
Henry's ears turned red
and Mudge's ears
turned inside out.

But one thing about them
was the same.
In the fall
Henry and Mudge liked
being together,
most of all.

Think and Respond

1 What are some things Henry and Mudge like to do
together in the fall?

2 In what ways are Henry and Mudge different?

3 What do you think Henry and Mudge will do in the
woods in the winter, spring, and summer?

4 What do you like to do in the fall?

5 Which strategy did you use to help you
read this story? Why?

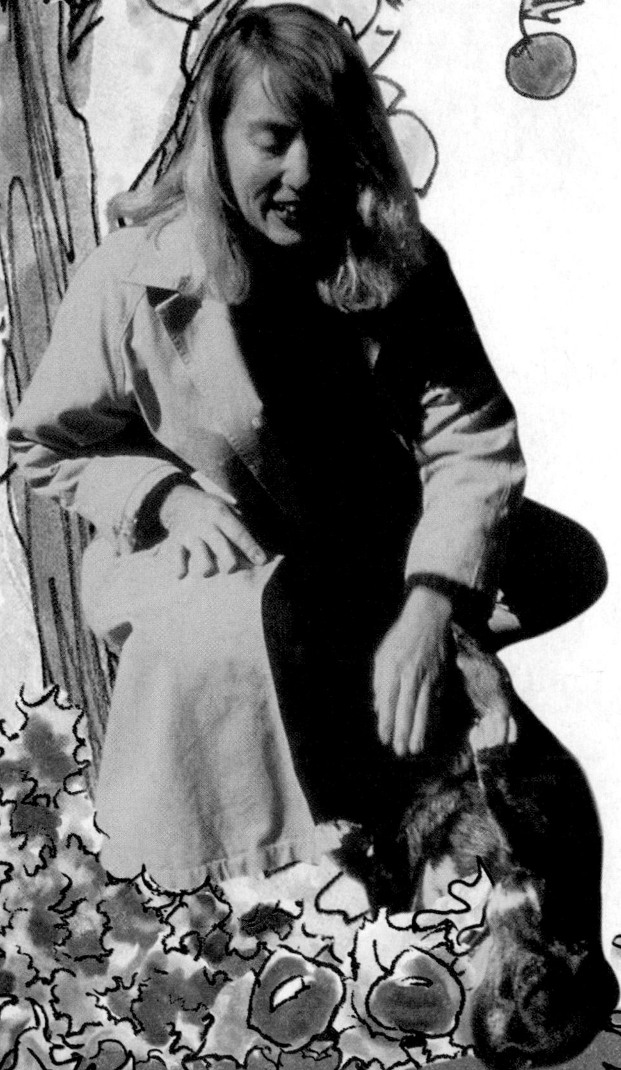

Meet the Author
Cynthia Rylant

Dear Readers,

I have two dogs named Martha Jane and Gracie Rose. Martha Jane is a big, white dog. She loves to eat pizza, chase tennis balls, and sleep on the couch. Gracie Rose is a little, short-legged dog. She loves to howl. I like to walk with my dogs just as Henry likes to go for walks with Mudge.

Cynthia Rylant

Visit *The Learning Site!*
www.harcourtschool.com

Meet the Illustrator
Suçie Stevenson

Dear Readers,

   I love drawing the pictures in the Henry and Mudge books. I have a new puppy named Merlin. He is an English mastiff dog, just like Mudge. Merlin is a lovely pup who drools only a little. When he is big, he will weigh 240 pounds and drool a lot!

Suçie Stevenson

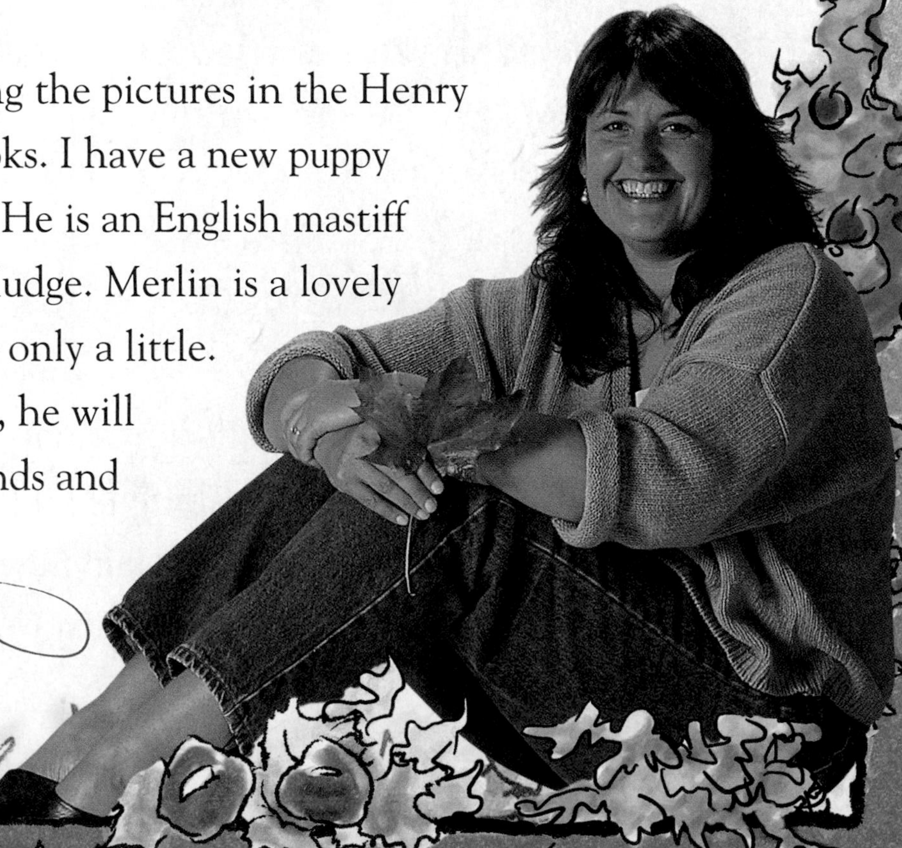

Making Connections

Compare Texts

1 Explain why "Henry and Mudge Under the Yellow Moon" is part of a theme called Being Me.

2 Think about the setting of "Henry and Mudge Under the Yellow Moon." How is it different from the setting of "The Mixed-Up Chameleon"?

3 How is the friendship between Henry and Mudge like the friendship between the girl and her dog in "Get Up and Go!"? Use examples from the stories to explain your answer.

Compare and Contrast

Write a paragraph that tells how Henry and Mudge are alike and different. Give examples from the story to explain how you know. Use a chart to make a list of your ideas.

Writing CONNECTION

Alike	Different
• Both have coats.	• Henry had to put his coat on, but Mudge grew his.

Show How They Grow

Henry and Mudge are growing up together, but their life cycles are different. Find out about the life cycle of dogs. Then make a fold-up book to help you show and tell about the different stages.

Giving Thanks

This story takes place in the fall. Thanksgiving takes place in the fall, too. Interview an older family member or neighbor. Ask how he or she celebrated Thanksgiving as a child, and how Thanksgiving has changed. Share what you find out with classmates.

97

Words That End in *ed*

Read this sentence from the story.

Henry <u>picked</u> apples and Mudge <u>licked</u> apples.

Read aloud the underlined words. Listen to the final sound in each word. Do you hear the sound for *t*? The letters *ed* stand for the sound for *t* in both words.

The words *hunted* and *mailed* also end in *ed*. Read each word aloud. What final sounds do you hear? The letters *ed* can also stand for the /ed/ sound, as in *hunted*, and the sound for *d* as in *mailed*.

Which word below ends with the sound for *d*? Which ends with the sound for *t*? Which ends with the /ed/ sound?

> **stayed**   **watched**   **painted**

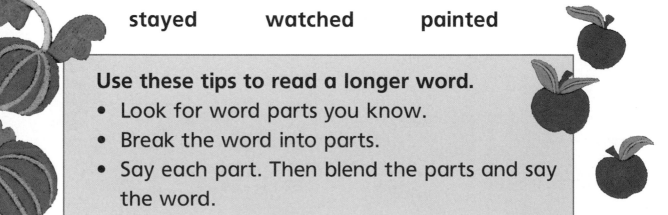

Use these tips to read a longer word.
- Look for word parts you know.
- Break the word into parts.
- Say each part. Then blend the parts and say the word.

Test Prep

Words That End in *ed*

Find the word in which the letters *ed* have the same sound they have in the first word.

Example: **floated**
- ○ backed
- ○ soaked
- ● drifted

Tip

Look at the underlined letters. What sound do they make when you sound out the word?

1. **locked**
- ◉ opened
- ○ sailed
- ○ asked

2. **rented**
- ○ touched
- ○ talked
- ○ hunted

3. **walked**
- ○ missed
- ○ mailed
- ○ cleaned

Phonics Skill

99

Vocabulary Power

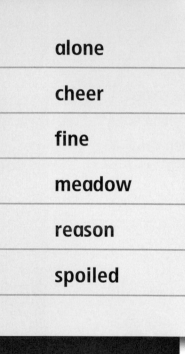

alone

cheer

fine

meadow

reason

spoiled

Today I took a walk. It's best not to walk **alone**, so I went with my dad.

We walked through the tall grass of the **meadow**. We saw many kinds of butterflies and flowers. It was a **fine** day for a walk because it was warm and sunny.

A little later, it started to rain. I thought our walk would be **spoiled** and we would have to go inside. I felt sad.

Suddenly it stopped raining. Dad smiled, but I didn't know the **reason**. Then I saw the rainbow. I smiled, too. Dad knew the rainbow would **cheer** me up.

Vocabulary-Writing CONNECTION

Write a list of things you could do to **cheer** up a friend who is sad.

101

ALA
Notable Book

Story

A story has characters, a setting, and a plot.

Look for

- a plot with a beginning, a middle, and an end.

- story events that happen in order.

Days With

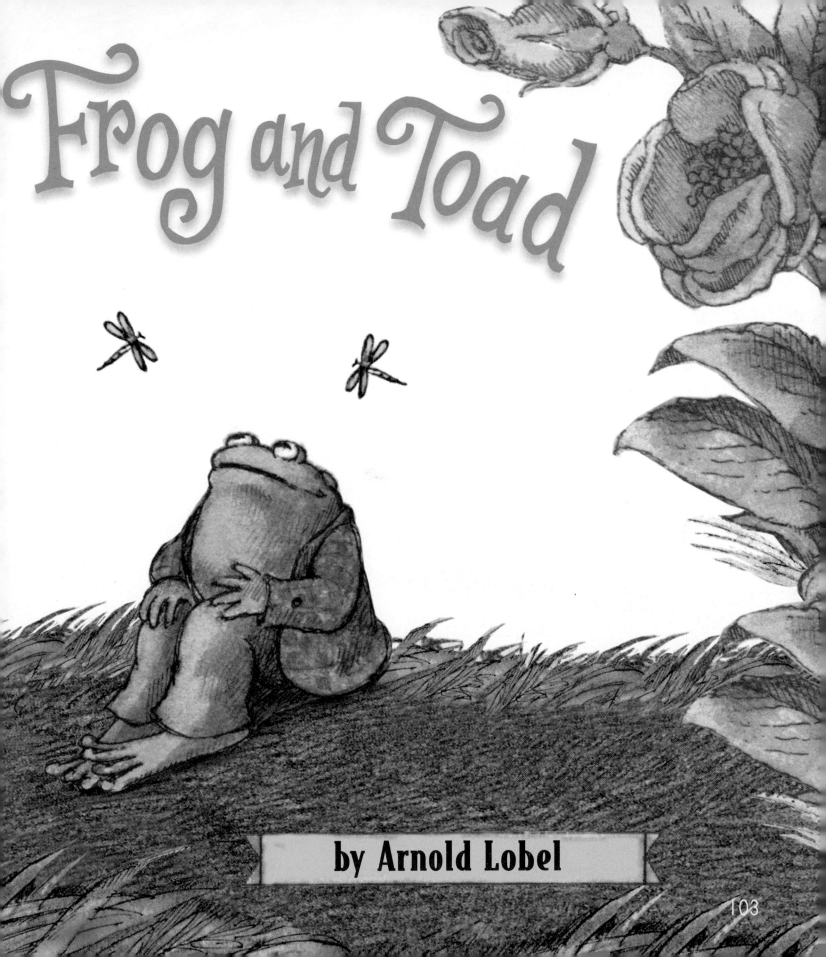

Frog and Toad

by Arnold Lobel

Alone

Toad went to Frog's house.

He found a note on the door.

The note said,

"Dear Toad, I am not at home.

I went out.

I want to be alone."

"Alone?" said Toad.

"Frog has me for a friend.

Why does he want to be alone?"

Toad looked through the windows.

He looked in the garden.

He did not see Frog.

Toad went to the woods.

Frog was not there.

He went to the meadow.

Frog was not there.

Toad went down to the river.

There was Frog.

He was sitting on an island

by himself.

"Poor Frog," said Toad.

"He must be very sad.

I will cheer him up."

Toad ran home.

He made sandwiches.

He made a pitcher of iced tea.

He put everything

in a basket.

Toad hurried

back to the river.

"Frog," hc shouted,

"it's me.

It's your best friend, Toad!"

Frog was too far away to hear.

Toad took off his jacket

and waved it like a flag.

Frog was too far away to see.

Toad shouted and waved,

but it was no use.

Frog sat on the island.

He did not see or hear Toad.

A turtle swam by.

Toad climbed on the turtle's back.

"Turtle," said Toad,

"carry me to the island.

Frog is there.

He wants to be alone."

"If Frog wants to be alone,"

said the turtle,

"why don't you leave him alone?"

"Maybe you are right," said Toad.

"Maybe Frog does not

want to see me.

Maybe he does not want me

to be his friend anymore."

"Yes, maybe," said the turtle

as he swam to the island.

"Frog!" cried Toad.

"I am sorry for all

the dumb things I do.

I am sorry for all

the silly things I say.

Please be my friend again!"

Toad slipped off the turtle.

With a splash, he fell in the river.

Frog pulled Toad

up onto the island.

Toad looked in the basket.

The sandwiches were wet.

The pitcher of iced tea was empty.

"Our lunch is spoiled," said Toad.

"I made it for you, Frog,

so that you would be happy."

"But Toad," said Frog.

"I *am* happy. I am very happy.

This morning

when I woke up

I felt good because

the sun was shining.

I felt good because

I was a frog.

And I felt good because

I have you for a friend.

I wanted to be alone.

I wanted to think about

how fine everything is."

"Oh," said Toad.

"I guess that is a very good reason

for wanting to be alone."

"Now," said Frog,

"I will be glad *not* to be alone.

Let's eat lunch."

Frog and Toad

stayed on the island

all afternoon.

They ate wet sandwiches

without iced tea.

They were two close friends

sitting alone together.

Think and Respond

1. What happens in this story?

2. How does the author show that Toad is a good friend to Frog?

3. Why did Toad try to **cheer** up Frog?

4. What do you like to think about when you are alone?

5. What strategies helped you read this story?

Arnold Lobel's children used to catch frogs and toads in the summertime. The toads made great pets. The Lobels put them in an aquarium, fed them, and gave them milk baths. Because Arnold Lobel was so interested in these animals, he wrote many stories about Frog and Toad.

Visit *The Learning Site!*
www.harcourtschool.com

Sometimes

Sometimes I like to be alone
And look up at the sky
And think my thoughts inside my head—
Just me, myself, and I.

by Mary Ann Hoberman
illustrated by Steve Johnson and Lou Fancher

Making Connections

Compare Texts

1. The title of this theme is Being Me. How is Frog being himself in this story?

2. Who are the characters in this story? How are they like Henry and Mudge?

3. What could Toad learn from reading the poem "Sometimes"?

A New Ending

Toad saw Frog sitting on an island. Frog was talking to Turtle.

Write a new ending for the story "Days With Frog and Toad." Tell what Frog and Toad do and say. Then share your story ending with a classmate. Talk about how your ending makes the story different.

Writing CONNECTION

Frog Poster

Make a poster that shows how a frog changes as it grows. Number and label your pictures. Then use your poster to tell how a frog changes over time.

Science CONNECTION

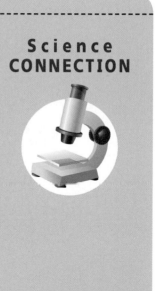

1. Tadpole

2.

A Famous Thinker

Marie Curie was a famous scientist. She discovered new materials that people can use. Find out more about Marie Curie. Write a paragraph telling who she was and what she discovered.

Social Studies CONNECTION

Compare and Contrast

When you **compare and contrast** stories, look at the settings, characters, and plots. Think about how they are the same and how they are different.

The story "Days With Frog and Toad" takes place in the country around lunchtime. Compare this setting with the setting of "Get Up and Go!"

Settings

"Days With Frog and Toad"	"Get Up and Go!"
• outdoors • in the country • during the day around lunchtime	• indoors • in a house • in the morning around breakfast time

Visit *The Learning Site!*
www.harcourtschool.com

See *Skills* and *Activities*

The two settings are different in all ways.

Now compare the settings of "Days With Frog and Toad" and "Henry and Mudge Under the Yellow Moon." How are they the same? How are they different?

Test Prep
Compare and Contrast

Read the paragraph. Then answer the questions.

A Surprising Day

My older brother and I went to the zoo. Suddenly it started raining really hard. We had no umbrellas, so we ran into the nearest building. It was dark and dry inside, yet there was as much water in there as outside. We had run into the aquarium building!

---

1. **What is the setting of the paragraph?**
   - ○ a farm
   - ○ a backyard
   - ○ the zoo

Tip

Reread the paragraph for the sentence that answers each question.

2. **How is what is inside the building the same as what is outside it?**
   - ○ There is water in both places.
   - ○ It is dark and dry in both places.
   - ○ The lions are kept indoors during the day.

▲ **Wilson Sat Alone**

amazing

clustered

gathered

raced

wandered

Vocabulary Power

Today was field day. After lunch, we **gathered** together on the basketball court. Mr. Harris told us about each event.

First, we had the 50-yard dash. All the runners **raced** as fast as they could to the finish line. Lee won by a few feet!

A crowd **clustered** around her. They all cheered and yelled out her name.

At the end of the day, we were tired. Slowly, we all **wandered** over to the awards table.

Mr. Harris had medals for everyone. I got the award for the longest jump. That was **amazing** to me!

Vocabulary–Writing CONNECTION

Have you ever done an **amazing** thing? Write about it. Tell what happened and why it was amazing.

125

wilson sat alone

by debra hess illustrated by diane greenseid

Genre

Realistic Fiction

Realistic fiction is a story with characters and events that are like people and events in real life.

Look for

- characters that have feelings that real people have.

- a setting that could be a real place.

Wilson

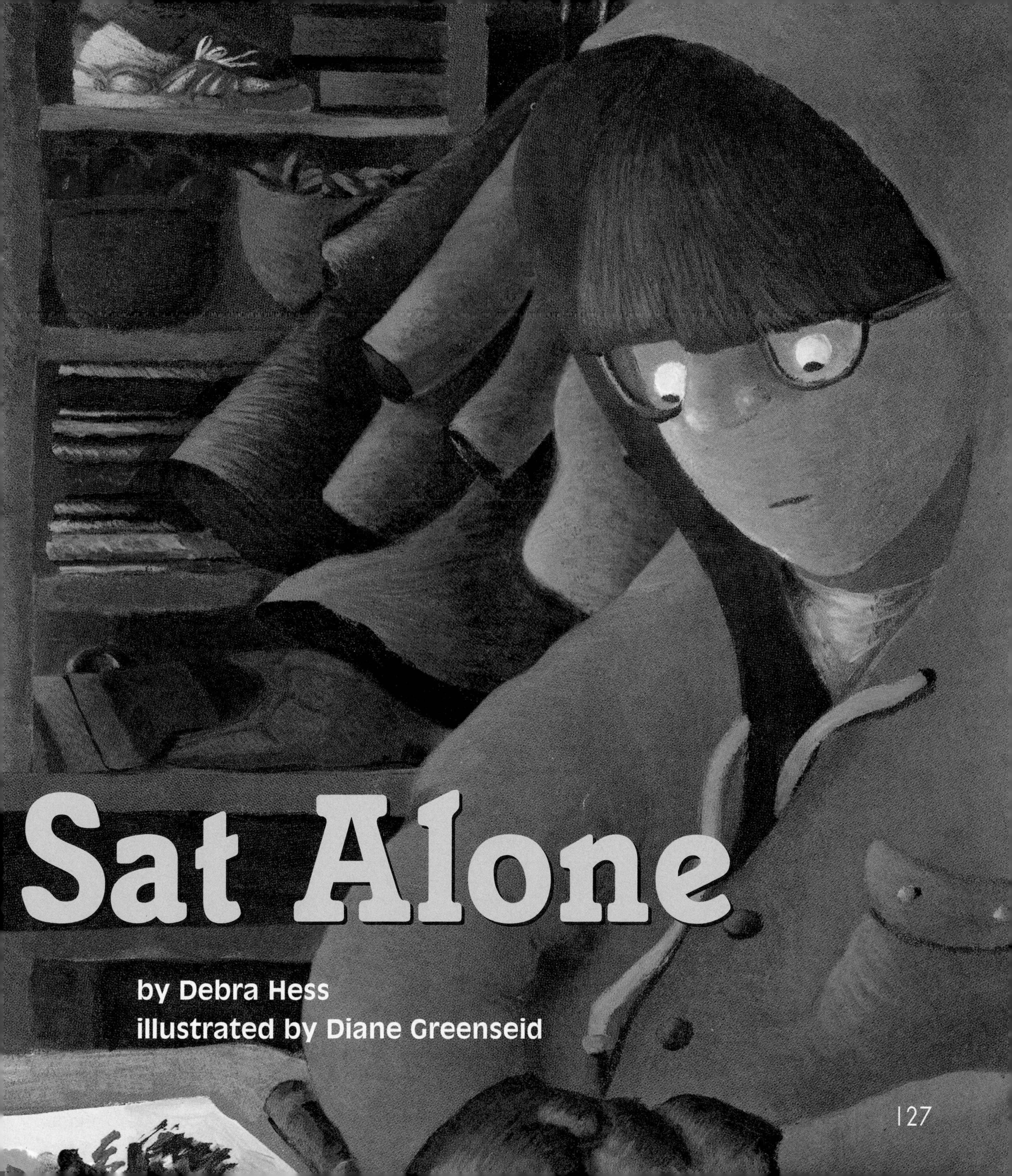

Sat Alone

by Debra Hess

illustrated by Diane Greenseid

On Mondays the children in Ms. Caraway's class pushed their desks together and sat in groups of six and seven.

Wilson sat alone.

At lunchtime,
when groups of
friends ate together
in the cafeteria,

Wilson ate alone.

At recess, when everyone
gathered for a kick ball game,
or played Cowboys and Indians,
or Dinosaurs and Monsters,

Wilson played alone.

And at the end of the day, when all the children rode the bus, or climbed into cars, or **wandered** home in packs of three or four . . .

Wilson walked alone.

On reading days, while everyone **clustered** into groups,

Wilson read alone.

On snow days, as Ben and Sam and Lucy and Meg
helped each other into their snowsuits,

Wilson dressed alone.

When the children built snowmen, and
threw snow, and laughed and screamed,
Wilson didn't laugh . . .

because he was alone.

One day a new girl came to school.

She said her name was Sara.

She smiled all the time.

She sat alone, and ate alone,

and read alone, and played alone.

But only for one day.

On her second day at school, Sara pushed
her desk into a group of other desks,
and ate with the other children,
and played Monsters in the snow,
and laughed.

And Wilson watched her from
where he sat,
alone.
He watched her all that day,
and all the next day, too.

And Sara saw him watching,
and raced across the snow,

and roared a monster roar at Wilson,
who sat alone.

"Don't do that!" said Lucy.

"Not to Wilson," called Sam.

"Why not?" asked Sara.

"He always sits alone," said Sam.

"He always plays alone," said Meg.

"He likes to be alone," said Ben.

And then
an amazing thing happened.

Wilson roared back.

Softly at first, and then louder,
and louder, and louder. . . .

It was the biggest, loudest,
grandest monster roar of all time.

And from that day on,
Wilson played with the other
children, and ate with them,
and sat with them, and read
with them, and walked
with them.

143

And Wilson was not alone anymore.

Think and Respond

❶ How does Wilson change in this story?

❷ Why are Sara and Wilson both important characters?

❸ Why do you think Wilson roars back?

❹ If your class **gathered** to play a game, how could you make sure no one was left out?

❺ What events did you think might happen next as you read this story?

Meet the Author and the Illustrator

Debra Hess

Debra Hess says that she almost never sat alone when she was a young girl. She talked to everyone just as Sara does.

Debra Hess lives in New York with her husband. She is the author of many plays and books for children.

Diane Greenseid

Diane Greenseid has illustrated many magazines and newsletters. This is the first time she has illustrated a children's book. She is known for using beautiful colors in her pictures.

Diane Greenseid lives in California.

Visit *The Learning Site!*
www.harcourtschool.com

145

Making Connections

Compare Texts

1 Why do you think "Wilson Sat Alone" is in a theme called Being Me?

2 Both Wilson and Frog from "Days With Frog and Toad" spend time alone. How are their reasons for being by themselves different?

3 How is Sara like Wilson? In what ways is she different?

Write a Letter

Imagine that a new child will join your class next week. Write a letter to make him or her feel welcome. Tell about things your class does that would be helpful for your new classmate to know.

Writing CONNECTION

October 11, 2004

Dear Rob,
I'm glad you are going to be in my class.

Good Citizenship

By being nice to Wilson, Sara shows good citizenship. What are other ways to show good citizenship? Work with classmates to add ideas to this list. Hang the list in your classroom where everyone can see it.

Use Good Citizenship
- Be kind to your classmates.
- Help others clean up.
- Wait your turn.

Pushing and Pulling

Sara pushes her desk to group it with other desks. Pushing or pulling something can make it move. Use a spring scale to find out how much force it takes to move things on your desk. Which object needs the most force to be moved?

Narrative Elements

Every story has a setting, characters, and a plot. The setting of "Wilson Sat Alone" is a school. The characters are Wilson and his classmates.

You can tell how a story character feels by reading what the character says and does.

At the Beginning	At the End
Wilson plays alone.	Wilson plays with others.
Wilson does not laugh.	Wilson laughs.
Wilson is not smiling.	Wilson smiles.

You can tell that Wilson feels sad and lonely at the beginning of the story. How does Wilson feel at the end?

Visit *The Learning Site!*
www.harcourtschool.com

See *Skills* and *Activities*

148

Test Prep
Narrative Elements

Read the paragraph. Then answer the questions.

> ### Dan's Answer
>
> Dan sat quietly in class. His hands were sweaty. He knew the answer, but he didn't want to raise his hand. Dan finally put his hand up. Then he stood and gave the answer. His friend patted him on the back. Dan smiled.

1. **How does Dan feel at the beginning of the story?**
    - ○ sad
    - ○ tired
    - ○ nervous
    - ○ bored

Tip
Reread the paragraph to make sure you understand the order of events.

2. **How does Dan feel at the end of the story?**
    - ○ hungry
    - ○ unhappy
    - ○ proud
    - ○ upset

Tip
Think how you would feel if you were Dan. Find the answer that is most like your idea.

Helping Hands

CONTENTS

▲ The Enormous Turnip

enormous

granddaughter

grew

planted

strong

turnip

Vocabulary Power

Here are Mrs. Smith and her **granddaughter**, Millie. They live next door to me.

Mrs. Smith has an **enormous** garden that covers almost her whole backyard. Last year, she **grew** vegetables, such as beans and carrots. She also **planted** many flowers in the soil.

Millie waters the garden and picks the vegetables. Mrs. Smith pulls weeds. She is **strong** enough to pull big weeds out of the ground by herself.

The other day, Mrs. Smith brought my family tomatoes, beans, and one giant **turnip**. I like living next door to Mrs. Smith!

Vocabulary–Writing CONNECTION

Imagine that you own an **enormous** garden. Write a paragraph that tells what kinds of plants you grow in it and why.

153

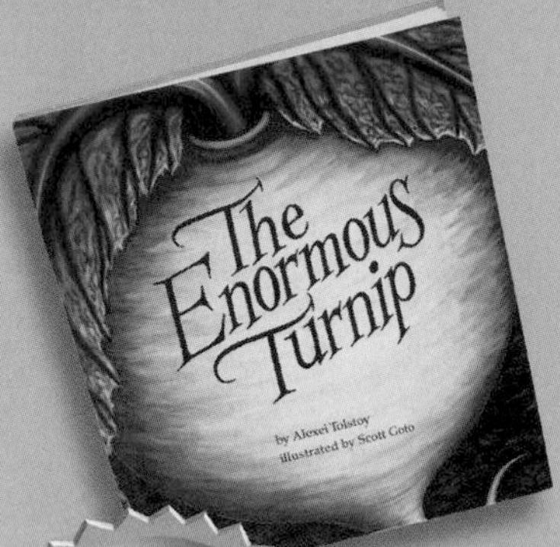

Award-Winning Author

Genre

Folktale

A folktale is a story that has been told for a long time by a group of people.

Look for

- **things that are much bigger than they could be in real life.**
- **events that happen over and over.**

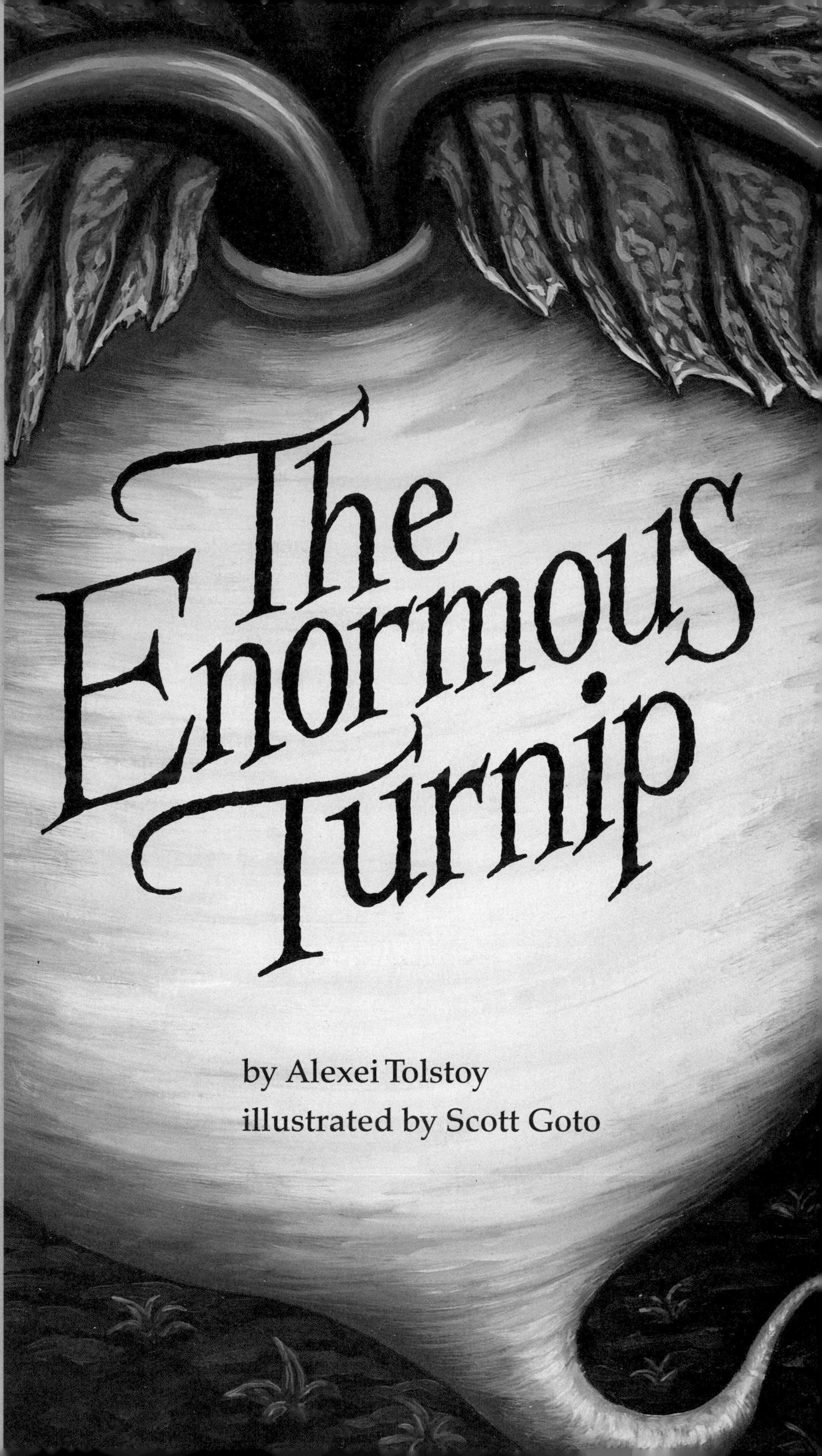

The Enormous Turnip

by Alexei Tolstoy
illustrated by Scott Goto

O nce upon a time an old man planted a little turnip and said: "Grow, grow, little turnip, grow sweet! Grow, grow, little turnip, grow strong!"

And the turnip grew up sweet and strong and big and enormous.

Then, one day, the old man went to pull it up. He pulled and pulled again, but he could not pull it up.

157

He called the old woman.
The old woman pulled the old man,
the old man pulled the turnip.
And they pulled and pulled again,
but they could not pull it up.

159

So the old woman called her granddaughter.
The granddaughter pulled the old woman,
the old woman pulled the old man,
the old man pulled the turnip.

And they pulled and pulled again, but they
could not pull it up.

The granddaughter called the black dog.
The black dog pulled the granddaughter,
the granddaughter pulled the old woman,
the old woman pulled the old man,
the old man pulled the turnip.

And they pulled and pulled again, but they could not pull it up.

The black dog called the cat.
The cat pulled the dog,
the dog pulled the granddaughter,
the granddaughter pulled the old woman,
the old woman pulled the old man,
the old man pulled the turnip.
And they pulled and pulled again, but still they could not pull it up.

The cat called the mouse.
The mouse pulled the cat,
the cat pulled the dog,
the dog pulled the granddaughter,
the granddaughter pulled the old woman,
the old woman pulled the old man,
the old man pulled the turnip.
    And they pulled and pulled again,

and up came the turnip at last.

Think and Respond

1 What happens in this story,
and how is teamwork important to it?

2 How would the story be different if
the old man did not call for help?

3 Why do you think the turnip grew to be so
strong, sweet, and enormous?

4 What do you do when you need help? Explain.

5 How can thinking about the order in which things
happen help you summarize the story?

About the Author

ALEXEI TOLSTOY was a writer in Russia. He wrote children's tales, as well as poems, plays, and stories for grown-ups. He also wrote science-fiction stories. One of them is about people who are going to the planet Mars.

Meet the Illustrator

SCOTT GOTO has been drawing since he was a child. His love of art makes him work very hard to be the best artist he can be. He loves listening to music, playing the guitar, and watching cartoons. Scott Goto also loves learning about history.

Visit *The Learning Site!*
www.harcourtschool.com

Making Connections

Compare Texts

1. Why do you think this folktale is in a theme called Helping Hands?

2. How are all the characters in this folktale alike? Explain your answer.

3. Think of a time when you needed help to do something. How many people did you ask? How did they help you?

Write Instructions

Write three steps that tell how to grow a plant. Number each step. Be sure your steps are in order.

Writing CONNECTION

All About a Plant

Grow a bean plant. Ask your teacher to help you. Draw a picture of the plant each day for two weeks. Then put the pictures in sequence. Talk with classmates about how your plant grew. Ask your classmates questions about their plants.

Thank You, Mr. Carver!

George Washington Carver was a scientist. He worked with peanut plants. He found more than 300 new ways to use them. Find out more about George Washington Carver. Give a report about his life and about how his work helped people.

Sequence

In "The Enormous Turnip," story events follow a time order, or **sequence**. The first event is at the beginning of the story, and the last event is at the end of the story. Time words such as *first*, *next*, *then*, *finally*, and *last* can help you figure out a story's sequence.

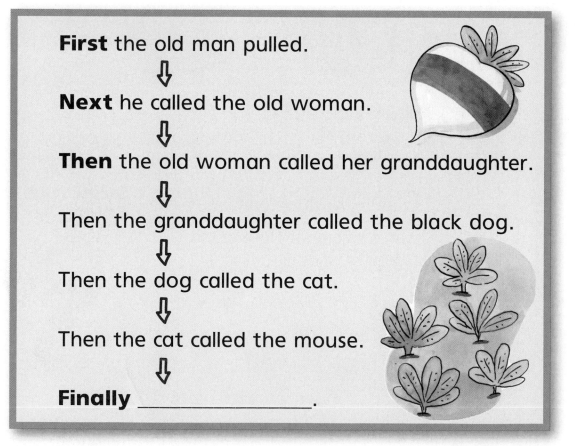

First the old man pulled.

⇩

Next he called the old woman.

⇩

Then the old woman called her granddaughter.

⇩

Then the granddaughter called the black dog.

⇩

Then the dog called the cat.

⇩

Then the cat called the mouse.

⇩

Finally _____.

What happens after the old man calls the old woman? What happens last in this sequence?

Test Prep
Sequence

Read the paragraph. Then complete the sentences.

Peter's Busy Mornings

Each morning at seven, Peter's mother wakes him up. First he gets out of bed. Next he brushes his hair and gets dressed. Then he eats his breakfast and brushes his teeth. Finally Peter goes outside to wait for the school bus.

1. **The first thing Peter does every morning is—**
   - ○ wait for the bus
   - ○ eat breakfast
   - ○ get out of bed
   - ○ wake up his brother

   Tip
   Be sure you understand whom the statement is about.

2. **The last thing Peter does before he leaves his house is—**
   - ○ get dressed
   - ○ eat his breakfast
   - ○ go to school
   - ○ brush his teeth

   Tip
   Look for time words such as *first*, *next*, and *last* as you read.

Vocabulary Power

alongside

chores

engine

simple

sprout

tool

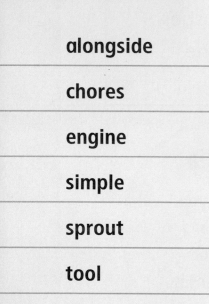

My family works together in the backyard each Sunday. We all have **chores**. These are jobs we do to keep our yard in good shape.

I work **alongside** my mom. I help her pull weeds from the garden. She makes it look **simple**, but I find it hard!

I watch my sister water the garden in spring. Sometimes we see a seed beginning to **sprout**.

My sister rakes the leaves. A rake is a handy **tool**. It makes her job easier.

Then my dad mows the lawn. Sometimes it's hard to get the mower's **engine** to start.

Vocabulary–Writing CONNECTION

Do people have **chores** in your family? Write about how each person helps out at home.

173

Words and photographs by George Ancona

Genre

Nonfiction:
Photo Essay

A photo essay tells about a topic using photographs and words.

Look for

- photographs that give important ideas about the topic.

- sentences that help you think about the photographs.

174

Helping Out

Words and photographs by George Ancona

Helping out can be as **simple** as being there to hand someone a **tool** when he needs it.

In early spring, you can help to plant seeds in the vegetable garden. Soon they will sprout and grow into many good things to eat.

You can turn some chores into fun, like washing the car on a hot summer's day.

Some jobs can be
dirty, like changing
the oil in the engine
of a car.

At school, a teacher needs
help keeping the classroom
neat and clean.

When you work alongside
an adult and do a good job,
you feel pretty big.

After you learn to do things well, you can begin to get paid for your work.

But the best thing about helping out is that it can bring two people closer together.

Think and Respond

1 How do the children in this selection help others?

2 Would this selection be as interesting without photographs? Why or why not?

3 Why do you think the author chose the photograph above to go with the last sentence?

4 What are some **simple** things you can do to help out at school?

5 What strategies helped you read this selection? When did you use them?

Meet the Author and Photographer
George Ancona

Dear Readers,

Some of the best times of my life were spent as a young boy helping out a grown-up. Sometimes I would work with my mother or father. At other times, I would help a neighbor or relative.

I decided to make this book after seeing what some young people do to help others. Perhaps you can think of more ways you can help those around you.

Visit *The Learning Site!*
www.harcourtschool.com

ALL JOIN IN

by Quentin Blake

When we're cleaning
up the house
We ALL JOIN IN

When we're trying
to catch a mouse
We ALL JOIN IN

When we've got some
tins of paint
We ALL JOIN IN

And when Granny's
going to faint
We ALL JOIN IN

And if Ferdinand decides to make
a chocolate fudge banana cake
What do we do? For goodness sake!

We ALL JOIN IN

Making Connections

Compare Texts

1. Why do you think "Helping Out" comes after "The Enormous Turnip"?

2. How did the photographs in "Helping Out" help you understand the words in the story?

3. Think about the poem "All Join In." How is it like "Helping Out"? How is it different?

Helping Can Be Simple

I was new at school, and I felt kind of lonely. Then Jake came over and invited me to play basketball with the other kids.

Think about a time when someone else helped you. What did that person do? Write a paragraph that tells what happened and how it made you feel. Share your story with classmates.

Writing CONNECTION

Helping the Environment

Think of one way that people can help the environment every day. Make a small poster that shows your idea. Share your idea with classmates.

Help save electricity!

Turn the lights off when you don't need them.

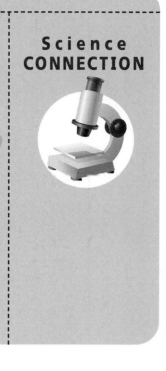

Super Helpers

Florence Nightingale, Susan B. Anthony, Andrew Carnegie, and Sojourner Truth all helped make the world a better place. Find out three facts about one of these people. Then give a short report to your classmates.

Social Studies CONNECTION

Susan B. Anthony was a super helper. She thought that women should have the same rights as men. She fought all her life to make sure that women got the right to vote.

Main Idea

The most important idea of a selection is called the **main idea**. Other sentences tell more about the main idea.

Read this paragraph.

On Friday afternoon, the second-grade classes did a nice job of cleaning the playground. Some children picked up trash. Others swept the sidewalks. The principal said that the playground looks like new!

To find the main idea, think about what the paragraph is mostly about.

Now think back to "Helping Out." What was the main idea? What were some of the details? Look for the main idea and details in other selections that you read.

Test Prep
Main Idea

Read the paragraph. Then answer the questions.

Fighting Fires
Firefighters are important in every community. They put out fires in homes, stores, and other places. They help people who are hurt in accidents. Many people are saved by firefighters every day.

1. **The main idea of the paragraph is —**
   - ○ Firefighters put out fires in stores.
   - ○ Firefighters are important to communities.
   - ○ Firefighters put out fires in homes.
   - ○ Firefighters help people in accidents.

Tip

Remember that the main idea is the most important idea of a selection.

2. **Which sentence does not tell more about the main idea?**
   - ○ Firefighters put out fires in different places.
   - ○ Firefighters help people who are hurt.
   - ○ Firefighters wear red hats.
   - ○ Firefighters save people each day.

▲ Mr. Putter and Tabby
Fly the Plane

cranes

directions

promise

twitch

worry

Vocabulary Power

I got a new toy car for my birthday. Before I played with it, I read the **directions** to find out how it worked.

I took the car outside to play with it. My dog, Rufus, came to see what I was doing. He sniffed at the car for a while. I watched his nose wiggle and **twitch**.

Then my brother wanted to play with the car. He made me a **promise** that he would be careful. "Don't **worry**," he said. "I'll take good care of it."

My brother decided to use his toy **cranes** to lift the car high into the air. It looked like fun. I decided to play, too!

Vocabulary–Writing CONNECTION

Write about a time when you made a **promise** to someone.

195

CYNTHIA RYLANT
Mr. Putter and Tabby
Fly the Plane

HOWARD

Award-Winning
Author

Genre

Realistic Fiction

Realistic fiction is a story about characters who act like real people.

Look for

- **a setting that could be a real place.**

- **events that could happen in the real world.**

Mr. Putter and Tabby

Fly the Plane

by Cynthia Rylant

illustrated by Arthur Howard

1

Toys

Mr. Putter loved toys.

He was old, and he knew

that he wasn't supposed

to love toys anymore.

But he did.

When Mr. Putter and his

fine cat, Tabby, drove into town,

they always stopped at the toy store.

Tabby was not happy at the toy store.
She was old, too,
and her nerves weren't as good
as they used to be.

The wind-ups made her twitch.
The pop-ups made her jump.

And anything that flew
gave her the hiccups.

But Tabby loved Mr. Putter,
so she put up with all of it.
While she twitched and jumped
and hiccuped, Mr. Putter
played with everything.
He played with the dump trucks.
He played with the cranes.
He played with the bear on the flying trapeze.

But most of all,

he played with the planes.

Ever since he was a boy
Mr. Putter had loved planes.
When he was young he had covered
his whole room with them.
Biplanes were his favorite,
but he also loved monoplanes
and seaplanes
and shiny ace Junkers.

He thought he might
really fly a plane one day.
But he never did.
So now he just looked
at toy planes
every chance he got.

One day when
Mr. Putter and Tabby
were in the toy store and Tabby
was hissing at a wind-up penguin,
Mr. Putter spotted a plane
he had never seen before.

It was white and red, with
two wings on each side
and a little flag on its tail.
It was the most beautiful biplane
he had ever seen.
And it had a radio control
so a person might really fly it.

Mr. Putter was in love.

He bought the little plane and put it

in the car with Tabby.

He told her not to worry.

He promised her a nice cup of tea

with lots of cream

and a warm English muffin.

But still she hiccuped all the way home.

The Little Plane

Mr. Putter kept his promise.

He gave Tabby tea with cream and a warm
English muffin.

Then together they went outside
to fly his new plane.

Tabby had stopped hiccuping,
but only because she was full of tea.
She still didn't like Mr. Putter's plane.
Mr. Putter sat on the grass
and read all the directions.

Then he put the plane on the
grass and stepped back
and pressed the start button.
But the plane did not start.
It just rolled over and died.
Tabby purred.

Mr. Putter ran to the little plane.

He set it right again.

He told it to be a good little plane.

He stepped back

and pressed the start button.

But the plane did not start.

It fell on its nose and died.

Tabby purred and purred.

Mr. Putter ran to the plane.

He brushed the dirt off its nose.

He told it to be a brave little plane.

He stepped back

and pressed the start button.

But the plane did not start.

One of its wings fell off

and it died.

Tabby purred and purred and purred.

But poor Mr. Putter was so sad.

He picked up his little biplane.

He told the plane that it was

all his fault.

He told it that he was an old man

and old men shouldn't have toys anyway.

He said he wasn't any

good at flying planes.

Tabby watched Mr. Putter.

She could see that he was sad.

Then she felt sad, too.

Tabby went to Mr. Putter

and rubbed herself against his legs.

She sat on his shoulder,

put her head by his,

and licked his nose.

This made Mr. Putter feel better.

He decided to try again.

He fixed the wing.

He set the little plane on the grass.

He told it that he and Tabby knew

it was the best plane in the world.

Then he pressed the start button.

The little plane choked.

The little plane coughed.

The little plane gagged.

But it didn't die.

It warmed up and began to sound better.

Then slowly, slowly, it rolled across the grass.

It picked up speed. . . .

And then it *flew*!

It flew high into the blue sky.

Mr. Putter cheered. Tabby purred and hiccuped.

Mr. Putter was finally flying a plane of his own!

Think and Respond

 How does Tabby help Mr. Putter fly his plane?

2 Why do you think the author tells about toys that make Tabby **worry**?

3 How can you tell that Mr. Putter and Tabby are good friends?

4 Think of your favorite toy. Why is it your favorite?

5 How did looking for word bits and parts help you read new words in this story?

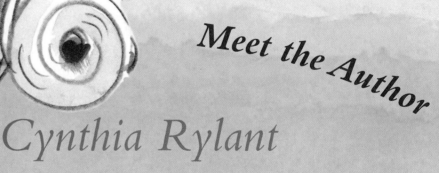

Cynthia Rylant

Dear Readers,

I love to write. I think that writing books adds beauty to the world. There are many other ways to add beauty, too, such as growing flowers, cooking delicious food, or raising sweet pets.

One of my pets is a cat named Blueberry. Blueberry likes only one thing—food!

♡ *Cynthia Rylant*

Arthur Howard

Dear Readers,

Before I illustrated this story, I thought a lot about Mr. Putter and Tabby. I asked myself what they would look like in a toy store or while flying a toy plane.

A lot of people ask me if I have a cat. I don't, but I love cats. I do have a pet hermit crab named Buster, though.

Visit *The Learning Site!*
www.harcourtschool.com

219

Jump for Health

by Tina Brigham

What is a good way to get exercise and help others at the same time? How about jumping rope? Eric Townes is a second-grade student from Lakeland, Florida. He and other children from his school jumped rope to raise money for a national group.

To get ready, Eric practiced jumping rope at home every day. The other children at his school practiced, too.

On the big day, family members and teachers went to the playground to watch. Some of the younger children had a hard time with their ropes, but they did their best. Eric helped cheer the younger children on.

At the end of the day, each child who jumped rope got an award. Eric also got a new jump rope! Best of all, he felt great knowing that he had helped others.

Making Connections

Compare Texts

1. Why do you think "Mr. Putter and Tabby Fly the Plane" follows "Helping Out"? What is the same about these selections?

2. How is Mr. Putter's problem like the old man's problem in "The Enormous Turnip"?

3. How is "Jump for Health" written differently from the way "Mr. Putter and Tabby Fly the Plane" is written?

A Toy Catalog

The Big Red Fire Engine has a ladder that goes up and down.

Help make a toy catalog for Mr. Putter. Draw pictures of toys that Mr. Putter would like. Below your pictures, write sentences that tell about your toys. Add your pictures to a class catalog.

Writing CONNECTION

Cat Facts

You can make cat trading cards. Find out about the life cycle of cats. Write each fact on an index card. On the back, draw a picture about the fact. Trade your cat cards with classmates.

Kittens open their eyes about a week after they are born.

Science CONNECTION

What Will You Be?

I want to be an astronaut and visit Mars.

When Mr. Putter was a boy, he dreamed of flying a plane. What special thing do you want to do when you are older? Make a poster that tells about your dream. Share your poster with classmates.

Social Studies CONNECTION

Common Abbreviations

An **abbreviation** is the short form of a word. Abbreviations usually start with a capital letter and end with a period.

You can abbreviate a person's title.
Mr. Yee   **Ms. Brown**
Mrs. Gupta   **Dr. Fuentes**

You read abbreviations in addresses.
Kelly Street → Kelly St.
Park Avenue → Park Ave.
Ocean Drive → Ocean Dr.

Kelly St.

The names of days and months can be abbreviated.
Sunday → Sun.   **January → Jan.**
Wednesday → Wed.   **November → Nov.**

You can abbreviate measurements, too.
1 foot → 1 ft.
1 inch → 1 in.
1 centimeter → 1 cm
1 kilogram → 1 kg

Most abbreviations for measurements don't have capital letters.

Test Prep

Common Abbreviations

Choose the correct abbreviation for each word.

Example: **Doctor**
- ○ dr.
- ○ Dr
- ● Dr.

Tip

Most abbreviations end with periods.

1. **foot**
- ○ ft.
- ○ ft
- ○ Ft

Tip

Remember that most measurement abbreviations don't start with capital letters.

2. **Mister**
- ○ Mr
- ○ Mr.
- ○ mr

3. **Street**
- ○ St.
- ○ St
- ○ st.

▲ Hedgehog Bakes
a Cake

batter

buttery

perfect

recipe

smeared

yellow cake

Vocabulary Power

Toshi wants to bake a cake. He needs to know how to make it, so he looks for a **recipe**.

First Toshi gathers flour, milk, and eggs. Then he mixes them together. He wants the **batter** to be smooth. He hopes the cake will be **perfect**.

Toshi has **smeared** some butter across the bottom of the pan. The butter will keep the cake from sticking. When he finishes, Toshi's hands are **buttery**, too.

Next he puts the batter in a pan and bakes it. Last he gives some cake to his friends to eat. Everyone agrees that this **yellow cake** is the best Toshi has ever made.

Vocabulary–Writing CONNECTION

Write a **recipe** for your favorite snack. List the things you need to gather. Remember to write the steps in order.

Genre

Story

A story has characters, a setting, and a plot.

Look for

- a plot with a beginning, a middle, and an end.

- story events that happen in order.

228

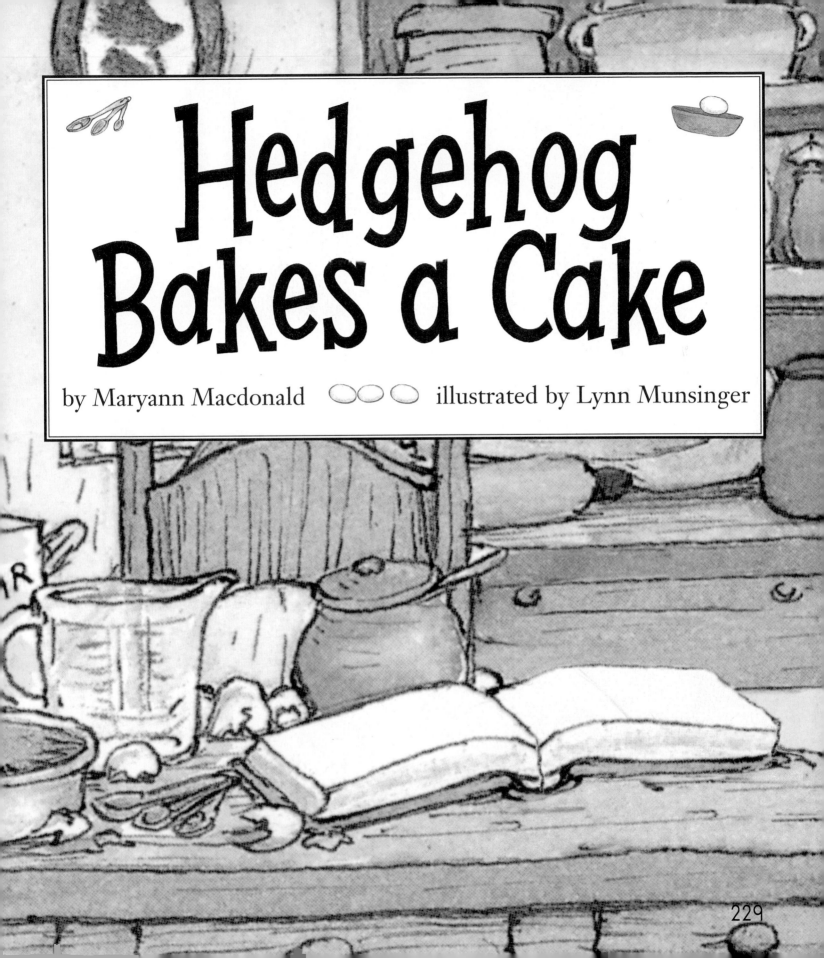

Hedgehog Bakes a Cake

by Maryann Macdonald   illustrated by Lynn Munsinger

Hedgehog was hungry for cake.
He found a yellow cake recipe.
"This one sounds easy," he said,
"and good, too."
Hedgehog took out the flour.

He took out the eggs and
the butter.

He was taking out the blue mixing bowl
when he heard a knock at the door.
It was Rabbit.
"Hello, Rabbit," said Hedgehog.
"I am making a cake."

"I will help you," said Rabbit.

"I am good at making cakes."

"Here is the recipe," said Hedgehog.

"You do not need this recipe," Rabbit said.

"I will show you what to do."

Rabbit took the flour.
He dumped it into the blue bowl.
He took the butter and dumped that in, too.
Then he dumped in the sugar.
"Now we will mix it," said Rabbit.

Mixing was hard work.
Rabbit mixed and mixed.
His arm began to hurt.
The batter was lumpy.
The sugar stuck to the sides of the bowl.
There was flour everywhere.
"I think someone is calling me,"
said Rabbit.
"You finish the mixing, Hedgehog.
I will come back
when the cake is ready."
Hedgehog shook his head.
The cake batter was a mess.

"What's the matter, Hedgehog?" Squirrel was at the door, looking in.

"I am making a cake," said Hedgehog.
"But it does not look very good."
"You need eggs," said Squirrel.
"I will put them in."
He cracked some eggs
and dropped them in.
Some shell fell in, too.

"A little bit of shell does not matter," said Squirrel. "Mix it all together." So Hedgehog mixed. The batter was more lumpy, but mixing was easier than before.

Owl stuck her head in the door.
"Baking?" she asked. "May I help?"
Hedgehog did not want more help.
But he didn't want to hurt Owl's feelings.

"You can butter the pan,"
said Hedgehog. Owl was happy.
She stuck her wing into the
butter. Then she smeared it
around the pan.

Owl turned on the oven
with her buttery feathers.
She turned it up as high
as it would go.
"The oven must be nice
and hot," she said.

"We have gotten very messy
helping you," said Squirrel.
"We will go home now and clean up.
Put the cake in the oven.
We will come back when it is ready."
Squirrel and Owl went home.

HEDGEHOG

Hedgehog looked at the kitchen.
There was sugar on the floor.
There was butter on the oven door.
And there was flour on everything.

Hedgehog dumped the cake batter into the garbage pail.

He locked the kitchen door and took out his recipe.

First Hedgehog measured the sugar.
He mixed it slowly with the butter.
Next he counted out three eggs
and cracked them into the bowl—
one, two, three.
Then he added the flour.

Hedgehog mixed everything together and poured it into Owl's buttery pan.
He turned down the heat and put the batter in the oven.

Then he cleaned up the kitchen.

Knock, knock, knock.
"Open the door, Hedgehog," called Rabbit.
"We can smell the cake, and we are getting hungry."
Hedgehog unlocked the door. The kitchen was clean.
The cake was cooling on a rack. And the table was set for a tea party.

The four friends sat down.

Hedgehog cut the cake.

They each ate one slice.

Then they each ate another slice.

"This is the best cake I have ever made," said Rabbit.

"Aren't you glad I showed you how to do it?"

"The eggs made it very rich," said Squirrel.

"And you can't taste the shell at all."

"It's perfect," said Owl.

"I set the oven just right."

"Thank you all for your help," said Hedgehog.

"Next time I will try to do it all by myself."

Think and Respond

1 What happens when Hedgehog lets his friends help him bake a cake?

2 How might the story have ended if Hedgehog had baked the batter Rabbit, Squirrel, and Owl helped mix?

3 Why doesn't Hedgehog tell his friends he baked a new **yellow cake**?

4 What do you like best about this story?

5 Which strategies did you use to help you read this story? Why?

Meet the Author

Maryann Macdonald

Maryann Macdonald has been around children most of her life. She grew up in a family of ten people. This helps her see things the way children do. As a young girl, Maryann Macdonald liked to listen to family stories. She soon began telling stories of her own. She published her first story when she was sixteen years old.

Meet the Illustrator

Lynn Munsinger

Lynn Munsinger illustrates magazines, schoolbooks, and greeting cards, but her favorite projects are children's books. She says, "I have wanted to be an artist for as long as I can remember. I really enjoy my work and cannot imagine doing anything else."

Visit *The Learning Site!*
www.harcourtschool.com

Hedgehog's Yellow Cake

by Maryann Macdonald

$\frac{3}{4}$ cup sugar

$\frac{1}{2}$ cup butter

3 eggs

$1\frac{1}{4}$ cups self-rising flour

1 teaspoon vanilla extract (optional)

1. Ask an adult to set the oven to 350°.

2. Butter a 9-inch round pan.

3. Mix butter and sugar together in a bowl.

4. Add eggs, one by one.

5. If desired, add vanilla.

6. Mix in flour.

7. Put batter into pan and bake for half an hour.

8. Eat warm with a glass of milk.

Making Connections

Compare Texts

1   Why do you think this story is in a theme about working together?

2   How is Hedgehog different from the old man in "The Enormous Turnip"?

3   Both "Hedgehog Bakes a Cake" and "Hedgehog's Yellow Cake" are about making cakes. Which selection would be more helpful if you wanted to make a real cake? Why?

You're Invited

October 11, 2002

Dear Robbie,

I am having a surprise birthday party for Erik. It will be at my house on November 4 at 3:00 P.M. I hope you will come.

Your friend,
Lori

Imagine that you are having a party. Write an invitation that tells when and where you are having the party. Write clearly.

Writing CONNECTION

250

How Much Does It Weigh?

Which weighs the most—a cup of milk, water, flour, or sugar? Use a measuring cup and a scale to find out. Make a chart to show your findings.

Science CONNECTION

How much does 1 cup weigh?	
Milk	
Water	
Flour	
Sugar	

Foods, Then and Now

Talk with older adults about foods they ate when they were children. What were their favorite foods? Did they eat foods then that people don't eat today? Are some foods prepared differently now than they were then? Tell a classmate what you found out.

Social Studies CONNECTION

Synonyms

Read these sentences.

"This recipe sounds <u>easy</u>," said Hedgehog.

"This recipe sounds <u>simple</u>," said Hedgehog.

How are the underlined words alike? They mean about the same thing. Words that have the same or almost the same meaning are called **synonyms**.

What are some synonyms for these words?

fast   happy   called

Now read these sentences.

The cake tasted <u>good</u>.

The cake tasted <u>delicious</u>.

Good and *delicious* are synonyms, but *delicious* is a stronger word than *good*. It has more meaning. Look at the synonym pairs below. Find the word that is stronger in each pair.

wonderful   nice

broke   smashed

tiny   small

Test Prep
Synonyms

Fill in the bubble next to the word that shows the correct answer.

Example: **Which word means the same as <u>big</u>?**
- ○ small
- ● large
- ○ alike
- ○ neat

1. **Which does *not* mean the same as <u>neat</u>?**
   - ○ clean
   - ○ tidy
   - ○ messy
   - ○ orderly

Tip

Watch out for the word *not* in test questions. If you miss it, you may choose the wrong answer.

2. **Which word is a synonym for <u>different</u>?**
   - ○ alike
   - ○ similar
   - ○ same
   - ○ unlike

Tip

Remember that synonyms are words with the same or almost the same meaning.

Vocabulary Power

announced

arrived

glum

members

rebuild

Last summer, we had a sand castle contest at the beach. I was on a team with three other people. The **members** of the team were Lila, Will, Karen, and me, Julio.

We worked hard on our castle until the judges got there. When the judges **arrived**, they looked first at another team's work.

Then a terrible thing happened. A huge wave knocked down our castle! We didn't want to give up. We decided to **rebuild**, but we would have to do it quickly.

A judge saw the **glum** looks on our faces as we worked. He knew what had happened, so he told us to take our time and to do our best.

Finally, the new castle was completed. The judges loudly **announced** the winners of the contest. We knew our extra work had been worth it when we won!

Vocabulary–Writing CONNECTION

When have you worked as part of a team? Tell who the team **members** were and what you did.

Lemonade

Genre

Realistic Fiction

Realistic fiction is a story with characters and events that are like people and events in real life.

Look for

- **a setting that could be a real place.**

- **events that could really happen.**

256

for Sale

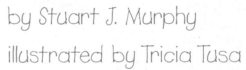

by Stuart J. Murphy
illustrated by Tricia Tusa

The members of the Elm Street Kids' Club were feeling glum.

"Our clubhouse is falling down, and our piggybank is empty," Meg said.

"I know how we can make some money," said Matthew. "Let's sell lemonade."

PRIVATE

Danny said, "I bet if we can sell about 30 or 40 cups each day for a week, we'll make enough money to fix our clubhouse. Let's keep track of our sales."

Sheri said, "I can make a bar graph. I'll list the
number of cups up the side like this. I'll show the
days of the week along the bottom like this."

On Monday they set up their corner stand. When people walked by, Petey, Meg's pet parrot, squawked "Lemonade for sale! Lemonade for sale!"

Matthew squeezed the lemons.

Meg mixed in some sugar.

Danny shook it up with ice and poured it into cups.

Sheri kept track of how many cups they sold.

Sheri announced, "We sold 30 cups today. I'll fill in the bar above Monday up to the 30 on the side."

"Not bad," said Danny.

"Not bad. Not bad," chattered Petey.

263

On Tuesday Petey squawked again, "Lemonade for sale! Lemonade for sale!" and more people came by.

Matthew squeezed more lemons.

Meg mixed in more sugar.

Danny shook it up with ice and poured it into more cups.

Sheri kept track of how many cups they sold.

Sheri shouted, "We sold 40 cups today. I'll fill in the bar above Tuesday up to the number 40. The bars show that our sales are going up."

"Things are looking good," said Meg.

"Looking good. Looking good," chattered Petey.

On Wednesday Petey squawked
"Lemonade for sale!" so many times that
most of the neighborhood stopped by.

Matthew squeezed
even more lemons.

Meg mixed in even
more sugar.

Danny shook it up with
ice and poured it into
even more cups.

Sheri kept track
of how many cups they sold.

Sheri yelled, "We sold 56 cups today.
I'll fill in Wednesday's bar up to a little
more than halfway between 50 and 60."

"That's great," shouted Matthew.
"That's great! That's great!"
bragged Petey.

They opened again on Thursday, but something was wrong. No matter how many times Petey squawked "Lemonade for sale!" hardly anyone stopped by.

Matthew squeezed just a few lemons.

Meg mixed in only a couple of spoonfuls of sugar.

Danny's ice melted while he waited.

Sheri kept track of the few cups that they sold.

Sheri said, "We sold only 24 cups today. Thursday's bar is way down low."

"There goes our clubhouse," said Danny sadly. Petey didn't make a sound.

269

"I think I know what's going on," said Matthew.
"Look!" He pointed down the street.
"There's someone juggling on that corner,
and everyone's going over there to watch."

"Let's check it out," said Meg.

Danny asked the juggler, "Who are you?"
"I'm Jed," said the juggler. "I just moved here."

Sheri had an idea. She whispered
something to Jed.

On Friday, Sheri arrived with Jed.

"Jed's going to juggle right next to our stand," Sheri said.

That day Petey squawked, Jed juggled, and more people came by than ever before.

Matthew squeezed loads of lemons.

Meg mixed in tons of sugar.

Danny shook it up with lots of ice and almost ran out of cups.

Sheri could hardly keep track
of how many cups they sold.

"We sold so many cups today
that our sales are over the top.
We have enough money to rebuild our clubhouse."

273

"Hooray!" they all shouted. "Jed! Jed!
Will you join our club?"

"You bet!" said Jed.

"You bet! You bet!" squawked Petey.

Think and Respond

 How did the children work together to **rebuild**
their clubhouse?

2 Reread page 273. How could you change the
ending of this story and still get a happy ending?

3 Why do you think the author used bar graphs
in the story?

4 If you were a member of a club, what could
you do to help raise money?

5 What strategies did you use to read this story?

Meet the Author and the Illustrator

Stuart J. Murphy

Stuart Murphy didn't enjoy math when he was young. But his feelings have changed. He now writes stories that show math ideas. He wants his stories to help children have fun as they learn math.

Stuart Murphy lives in Illinois with his wife. He loves to plan vacations—and to take them, too!

Tricia Tusa

Tricia Tusa has been a writer and illustrator of children's books since 1984. She is also an art therapist. She uses art to help children who are sad or hurt. She likes to show in her books that "it's okay to be different." Tricia Tusa lives in Houston, Texas.

Visit *The Learning Site!*
www.harcourtschool.com

275

Lemonade

Lemons all are yellow.

Lemons are afraid.

So squeeze a lemon gently

And give a lemonade.

by Pyke Johnson, Jr.

Making Connections

Compare Texts

1   Why is "Lemonade for Sale" part of the theme Helping Hands?

2   How is the way the characters in "Lemonade for Sale" work together different from the way the characters in "Hedgehog Bakes a Cake" work together?

3   Tell how the writing in "Lemonade for Sale" is different from the writing in the poem "Lemonade."

Read All About It!

Write notes for a newspaper story about the new lemonade stand in town. Include the 5 *W*'s: *who, what, when, where,* and *why.*

Writing
CONNECTION

Who	
What	
When	
Where	
Why	

Drink Graph

**Math
CONNECTION**

What do your classmates like to drink? Ask each classmate which drink he or she likes best—milk, lemonade, or water. Then make a bar graph to show your results.

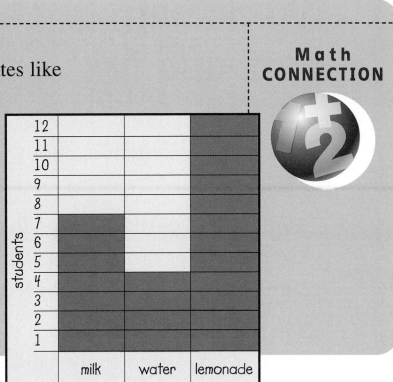

students	milk	water	lemonade
12			
11			
10			
9			
8			
7			
6			
5			
4			
3			
2			
1			

What Are You Selling?

**Social Studies
CONNECTION**

If you could make and sell something, what would it be? Create an ad for it. Draw your product, and write sentences that tell why people should buy it. Read your ad to classmates.

Dana's Delicious Cookies!

Dana's chocolate chip cookies taste great. They make your mouth water even before you eat them!

More than ten chips are in every cookie!

Words with *ar, arm,* and *ark*

Read these sentences about the story "Lemonade for Sale."

Someone is getting out of the <u>dark</u> <u>car</u>.

Sheri lifts her <u>arm</u> to <u>mark</u> the <u>bar</u> graph.

Did they buy their lemons from a <u>farm</u>?

Say the underlined words *dark, car, arm, mark, bar,* and *farm*. Listen to the ending of each word. Which words end the same way?

- ar	-arm	-ark
car	arm	dark
bar	farm	mark

Here are some longer words. Use what you know about word parts to help you read these words.

farming	darken	remark
charming	parked	farther

Use these tips to read a longer word.

- Look for word parts you know.
- Break the word into parts.
- Say each part. Then blend the parts and say the word.

Test Prep

Words with *ar*, *arm*, and *ark*

Find the word that has the same sound as the underlined letters in the first word.

Example: **c<u>ar</u>**

● part
○ pare
○ care

1.   **sp<u>ar</u>kling**
   ○ darken
   ○ calling
   ○ armor

Tip

Break the word into syllables when you sound it out.

2.   **<u>far</u>**
   ○ car
   ○ word
   ○ stare

Tip

Read all the choices before you pick one.

3.   **un<u>harm</u>ed**
   ○ story
   ○ bear
   ○ alarming

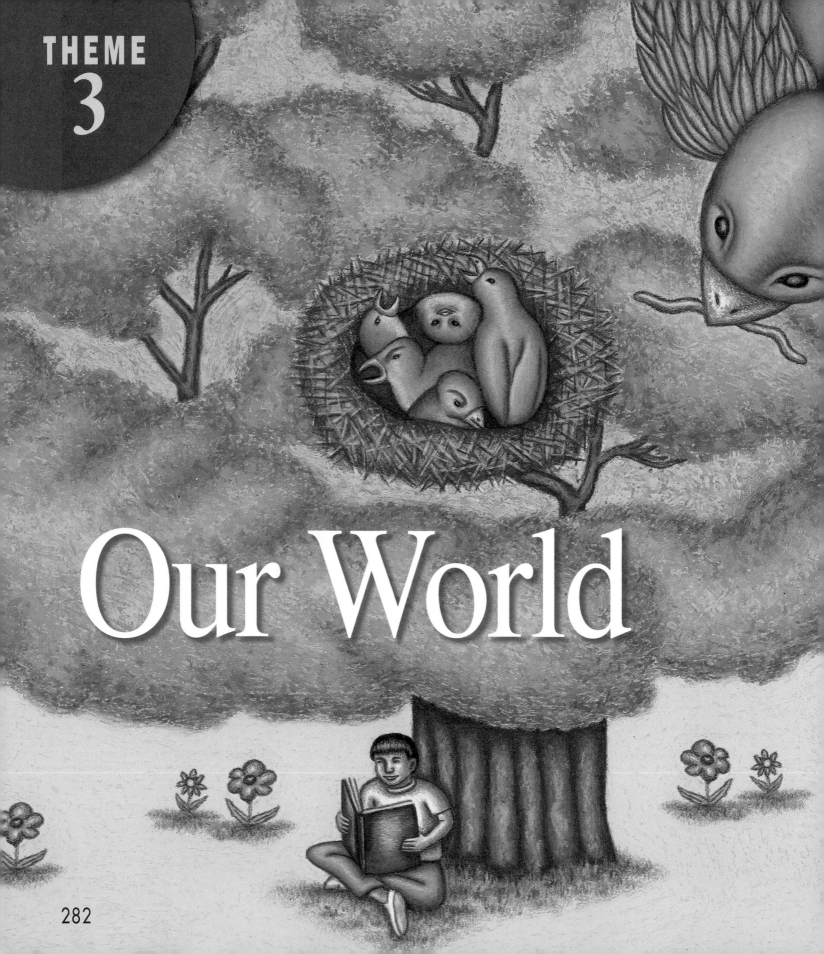

Our World

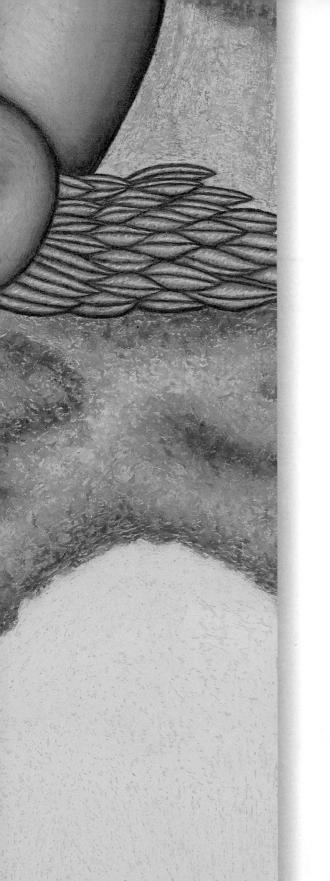

CONTENTS

▲ Johnny Appleseed

Vocabulary Power

frontier

nearby

orchards

survive

tame

wild

Howdy! This is the **frontier**, a place where few people live. It is hard to **survive** here, and we must work long hours to stay alive. This fence keeps **wild** animals, such as deer, from eating our garden.

Our cabin is in the perfect spot! A river is **nearby**, so we can get water right here. Do you see the **orchards** on the hill? Those fruit trees have hundreds of apples, which we can pick for food.

We asked Ma, "If we **tame** the deer to be like pets, can we keep them?"

Vocabulary–Writing CONNECTION

Why do you think it was hard for people to **survive** on the **frontier**? Write two or three sentences that tell your ideas.

Johnny

Characters

Narrator

Chorus, five girls and five boys (**Johnny's** ten half-sisters and half-brothers)

Johnny Appleseed, age 30

Frontier Father

Frontier Mother

Frontier Girl

Frontier Boy

Young Wolf and **Ten Horses**, two American Indians, friends of **Johnny Appleseed**

Johnny Appleseed, age 70

Appleseed

**an American Legend
adapted by Pleasant deSpain
illustrated by Victoria Raymond**

Scene One

Time: *Long ago.*

Setting: *Clearing in the woods.* **Narrator** *sits on a hollow log.* **Johnny**, *age 30, barefoot and wearing a stew pot on his head, munches on an apple.* **Chorus** *is nearby.*

Narrator: This is the story of John Chapman, a true American hero. You might know him as Johnny Appleseed. Johnny was born in Massachusetts a long time ago. He had ten half-brothers and half-sisters.

Chorus: (*waves*) That's us!

Narrator: When Johnny was a boy, many of his neighbors were moving out west. They were pioneers on the wild frontier. Johnny decided that when he became a man, he would also go out west. He wanted to plant apple seeds everywhere he went. That way, the pioneers would have apples to eat at their new homes.

Narrator: Johnny left home at age 23.

Chorus: What did he take with him?

Narrator: He took a pot for cooking and a sack of apple seeds. He walked and walked and he planted and planted.

Chorus: He walked and walked and he planted and planted.

Narrator: 'Cause he had itchy feet!

Chorus: 'Cause he had itchy feet!

Narrator: Now Johnny is 30 years old. He hates to wear shoes, and he likes to sleep outdoors. He likes animals as much as he does people. He has been walking west and planting apple orchards for seven years now.

Chorus: Apple juice and apple butter.
Apple sauce and apple cobbler.
My, oh my, sweet apple pie!
Yummmmmmmmmmmm!

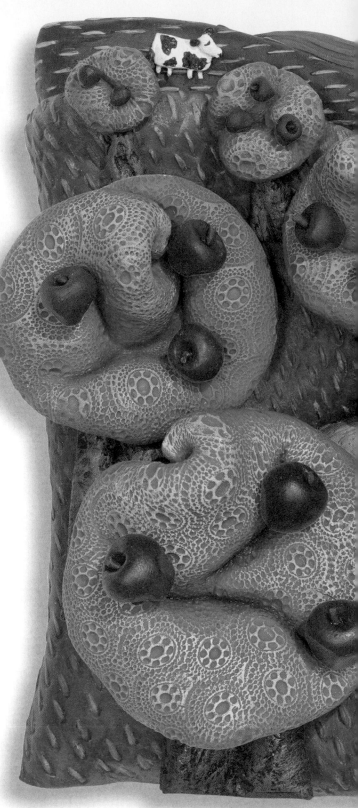

291

*(**Frontier Family** walks into the clearing.)*

Johnny: Howdy, folks! Come on over and rest a spell.

Frontier Girl: Pa, that man is wearing a pot on his head.

Frontier Boy: He looks strange, Ma!

Johnny: Don't be scared. People call me Johnny Appleseed.

Frontier Father: *(surprised)* We heard about you in Pennsylvania, and now here you are in Ohio.

Johnny: It's these itchy feet of mine. I have to keep moving west.

Frontier Mother: You planted all the apple trees we have seen along the way.

Frontier Father: That's hard work. Who pays you?

Johnny: *(laughs)* Nature does. I plant the orchards before folks move west so the apples are already growing when they arrive. The apples are nature's gift, and I just pass it along.

293

Frontier Girl: Pa says we are going to build a cabin and live here.

Frontier Boy: Where is your cabin, Johnny?

Johnny: (*laughs*) All around you. The earth is my floor, and the sky is my roof. The sun and wind and rain are my friends. This stew pot keeps my head dry, and wherever I go, I have all I need.

Frontier Mother: Don't you get cold?

Frontier Girl: Don't you get scared?

Frontier Boy: Don't you get lonely?

Johnny: Yes, yes, and yes. That's part of living outdoors, but I make friends wherever I go. My Indian friends have taught me how to survive in the great outdoors.

*(**Young Wolf** and **Ten Horses** walk into the clearing.)*

Johnny: Hello, Young Wolf and Ten Horses.

Young Wolf: Hello, Tree Planter. Who are these strangers?

Johnny: Meet my new friends. They came by wagon all the way from New England. They want to build a cabin here. They are good folks and good neighbors.

Frontier Father: Johnny's right. We promise to be good neighbors.

Young Wolf: Tree Planter always speaks the truth. Welcome, friends!

*(**Frontier Family** cheers.)*

Ten Horses: Be careful of the she-bear, Tree Planter.

*(**Young Wolf** and **Ten Horses** walk off.)*

Frontier Children: *(frightened)* The she-bear?

Johnny: Yes, I've heard her growl a time or two, but I get along with bears just fine.

Frontier Father: We must get back to the wagon. Thanks for everything, Johnny Appleseed.

*(**Frontier Family** walks off through the trees.)*

Johnny: *(yawns and stretches)* I'm so tired. I'll sleep in this hollow log tonight and finish planting the apple orchard tomorrow.

(**Johnny** *starts to crawl into the log.*)

Narrator: *(roars like a bear)* Grrrrrrrrrrr!

Johnny: *(startled)* I'm sorry Mrs. Bear!
I didn't know that this was your bed, too.
I'll sleep under the tree over there. You have
sweet dreams, you hear?

Narrator: *(growls warmly)* Mmmmm!

*(**Johnny** sits under tree and sleeps.)*

Scene Two

Time: *Many years later.*

Setting: ***Narrator*** *and* **Chorus** *are standing in an apple orchard.*

Narrator: Johnny Appleseed is now 70 years old. He's walked a long way, and he's still going.

Chorus: Apple juice and apple butter.
Apple sauce and apple cobbler.
My, oh my, sweet apple pie!
Yummmmmmmmmmmmm!

(**Johnny,** with a long white beard and a pot on his head, walks into the orchard. He carries a bag of seeds over his shoulder and a bright red apple in his hand.)

Chorus Girls: How far did you walk, Johnny?

Johnny: Must be thousands of miles.

Chorus Boys: How long did it take?

Johnny: It took almost fifty years.

Chorus Boys: How many trees did you plant?

Johnny: Too many to count.

Chorus Girls: Who eats all the apples?

Johnny: The good folks who move out west looking for a better life.

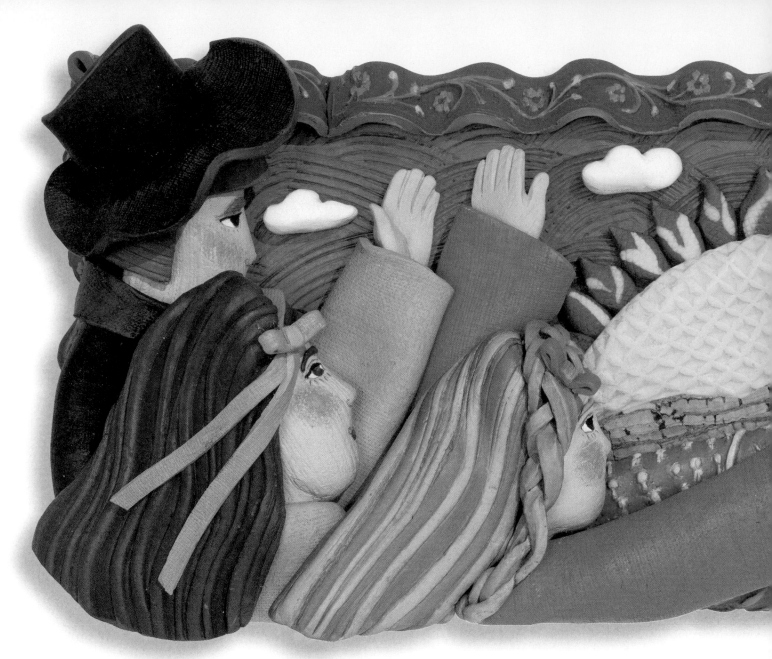

Chorus: Do you still have itchy feet?

Johnny: *(laughs)* I was born with itchy feet. Got to keep on going, that's what I always say. This great new country needs lots of apples. They help us grow strong and healthy.

*(**Johnny** bites into apple and slowly begins to walk away.)*

Chorus: Good-bye, Johnny Appleseed.

Johnny: May you always be blessed with apples.

Chorus Girls: Thank you, Johnny Appleseed.

Chorus Boys: Be careful of the bears.

(**Johnny** *waves good-bye and walks out of sight.*)

Narrator: John Chapman died when he was 71 years old. We will never forget this pioneer and American hero.

Chorus Girls: Appleseed Johnny, Johnny Appleseed. John Chapman was his real name. The wild frontier he helped to tame.

Chorus Boys: He planted apple seeds, which grew into trees. This was his story. Everyone clap now, please.

*(**Chorus** bows.)*

The End

Think and Respond

1 What did you learn about Johnny Appleseed and his travels on the **frontier**?

2 What is the setting of this play? Why is it important?

3 Why do you think the author used a narrator?

4 Would you like to live outdoors as Johnny Appleseed did? Why or why not?

5 What strategies did you use to help you read?

Meet the Author
Pleasant deSpain

Pleasant deSpain wrote his first story when he was eight years old. He's been writing and telling stories ever since. When Pleasant deSpain visits schools, he likes to act out stories in front of a class. That's why he wrote "Johnny Appleseed" as a play.

Meet the Illustrator
Victoria Raymond

Victoria Raymond uses clay to make her illustrations. She twists, pulls, rolls, and pounds the clay to give it the shape she wants. She uses the bark or leaves from trees to make impressions, or marks, in the clay. Like Johnny Appleseed, she and her family are moving out west.

305

Genre
Poetry

The Seed

How does it know,
this little seed,
if it is to grow
to a flower or weed,

if it is to be
a vine or shoot,
or grow to a tree
with a long deep root?

A seed is so small
where do you suppose
it stores up all
of the things it knows?

by Aileen Fisher
illustrated by Simon James

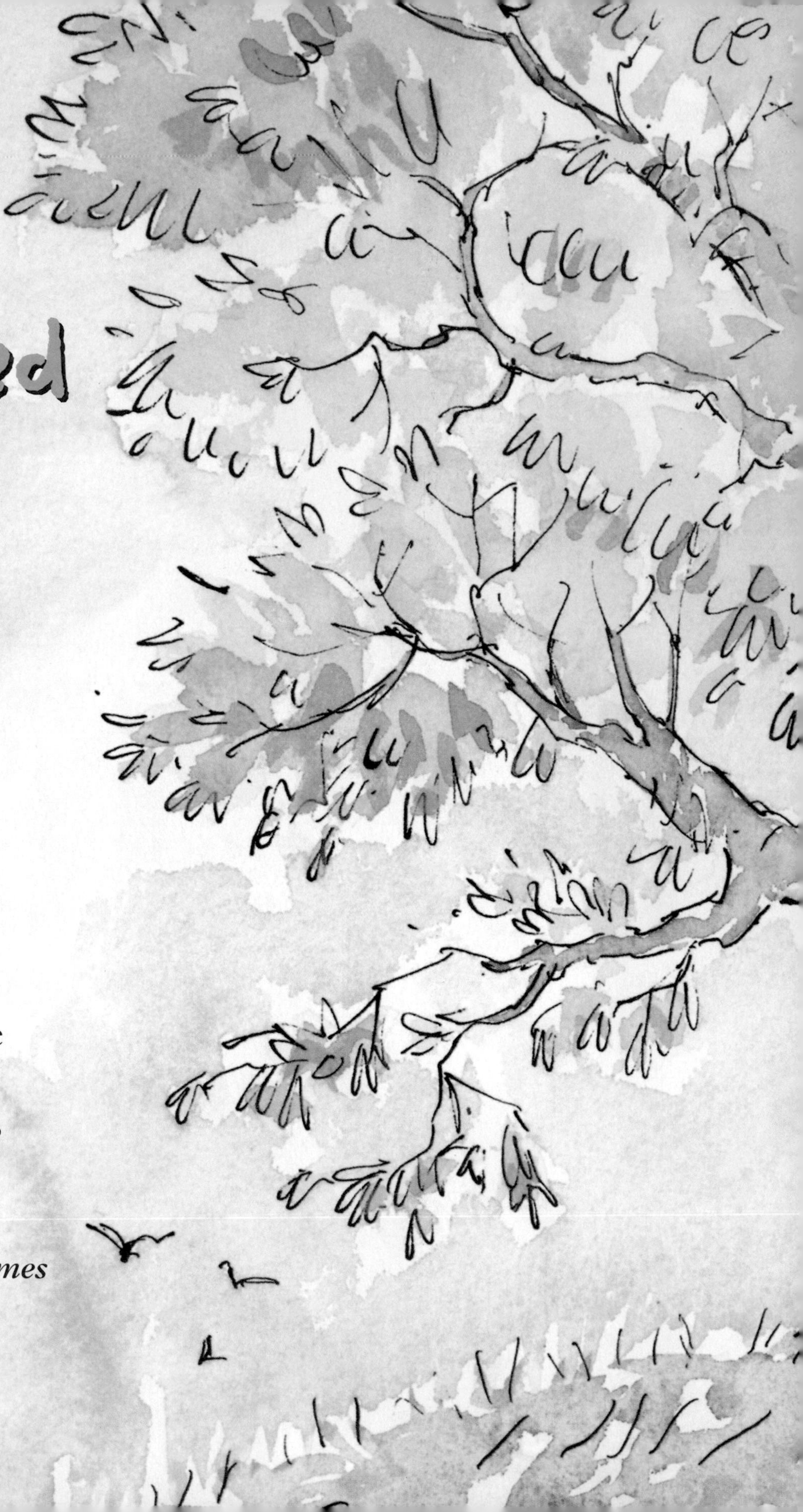

▲ Johnny Appleseed

Making Connections

Compare Texts

1   This theme is called Our World. Based on "Johnny Appleseed," what do you think this theme will be about?

2   How did Johnny Appleseed change in Scene Two? How did he stay the same?

3   Do you think a play is the best way to tell the true story of Johnny Appleseed? Why? What are other ways to write a true story?

Write About a Person

My brother is my hero. He teaches me new games.

Johnny Appleseed was an American hero because he helped the pioneers. Think about someone who is a hero to you. Draw a picture of that person. Write sentences that tell why that person is a hero.

Writing
CONNECTION

Make a Chart

The apple is one of the most popular fruits in the world. Find facts about apples. Then make a chart that helps you share the facts with others. You may want to look for answers to these questions:

- What kinds of apples are there?
- What colors are apples?
- Where do apples grow?

Apples!

Kind of Apple	Color
Roman	

Fact Cards

Johnny Appleseed was born in 1774. Make three fact cards that tell about events that happened in the United States when Johnny Appleseed was young. Use your social studies book and other books to find information. Draw pictures to go with your facts. Then share your fact cards.

USA

The United States began as thirteen colonies.

▲ Johnny Appleseed

Words with *ear* and *eer*

Read these sentences about Johnny Appleseed.
Johnny Appleseed slept outdoors with rabbits, squirrels, and <u>deer</u>.
Johnny Appleseed died when he was 71 <u>years</u> old.

Say the underlined words *deer* and *years*. Do you hear the same sound in each word? The letters *eer* and *ear* both stand for that sound.

Look at the two words below. What do you notice about *appear* and *pioneer* that could help you read the words?

appear   **pioneer**

Here are some longer words. Use what you know about word parts to help you read these words.

clearing   **nearby**   **volunteer**
steering   **dearest**   **nearer**

> **You can use these tips to read longer words.**
> • Look for word parts you know.
> • Break the word into parts.
> • Say each part. Then blend the parts and say the word.

310

Test Prep

Words with ear and eer

Find the word that has the same sound as the underlined letters in the first word.

Example: **y<u>ear</u>s**

- ○ press
- ● deer
- ○ heard

1. **p<u>eer</u>**
   - ○ pair
   - ○ poor
   - ○ hear

2. **pion<u>eer</u>**
   - ○ under
   - ○ dearly
   - ○ airplane

Tip

Read all the words. Listen closely for the sound you hear in the first word.

▲ From Seed to Plant

Vocabulary Power

beautiful

nutrition

protects

ripens

streams

Fruit grows all around the world. How many kinds of fruit can you name?

Fruit trees grow well near **streams** or small rivers. All plants need water to grow.

Fruits such as oranges and bananas are full of **nutrition**. They make a healthful snack anytime.

Fruit tastes best after it **ripens**. Which banana is ripe?

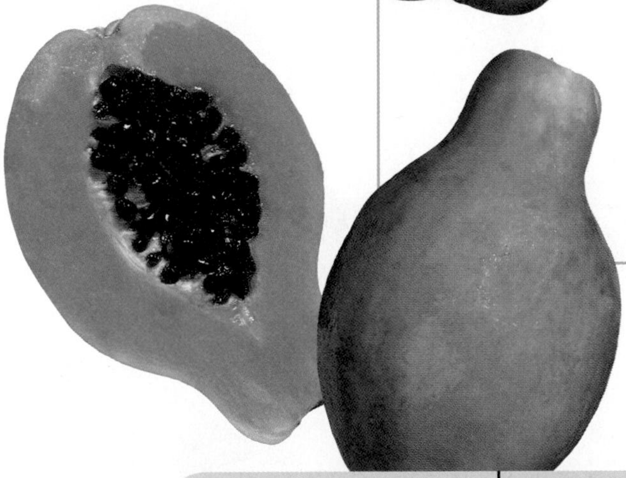

Many fruits are **beautiful**, with bright, pretty colors. A fruit also has a job to do. It **protects** the seeds inside it.

Vocabulary–Writing CONNECTION

Write about your favorite fruit. Describe how it looks, feels, smells, and tastes after it **ripens**.

313

From Seed to Plant

by Gail Gibbons

oak tree

sunflower

Most plants make seeds. A seed contains the beginning of a new plant. Seeds are different shapes, sizes and colors.

All seeds grow into the same kind of plant that made them.

apple tree

dandelion

zinnia

aster

Many plants grow flowers. Flowers are
where most seeds begin.

petal

The sticky part at the top of the pistil is the **stigma.**

Stamens make yellow powder called **pollen.**

In the center of the flower is the **pistil.**

The parts of the flower around the pistil are the **stamens.**

At the bottom of the pistil are tiny egg cells called **ovules.**

sepal

stem

A flower is made up of many parts.

Before a seed can begin to grow, a grain of pollen from the stamen must land on the stigma at the top of the pistil of a flower like itself. This is called pollination.

Pollination happens in different ways.
Often, wind blows pollen from flower to flower.

Bees, other insects and hummingbirds help pollinate, too. While they visit flowers for their sweet juice, called nectar, pollen rubs onto their bodies.

Then they carry the pollen to another flower where it comes off onto its pistil.

pollen

pistil

pollen

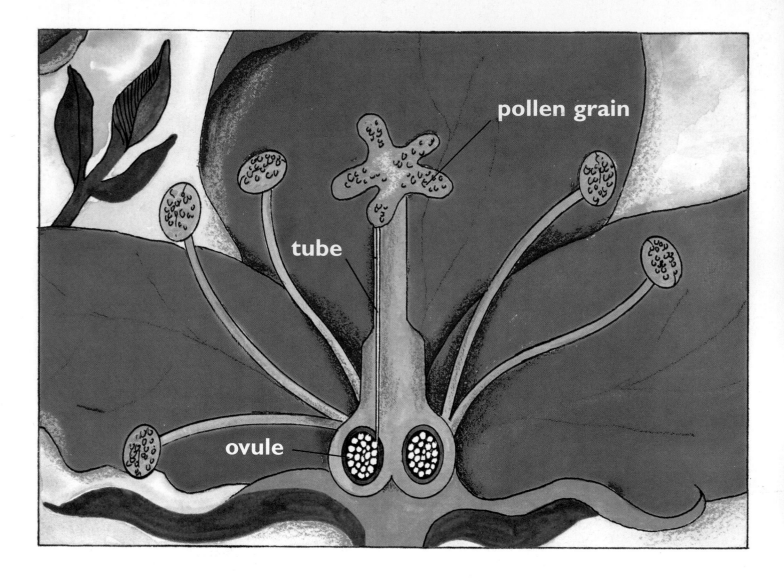

If a pollen grain from a flower lands on the pistil of the same kind of flower, it grows a long tube through the pistil into an ovule. This is the beginning of a seed.

fruit

pod

The seeds grow inside the flower, even as the flower begins to die. As the seeds become bigger, a fruit or pod grows around them. The fruit or pod protects the seeds.

When the fruit or pod ripens, it breaks open. The seeds are ready to become new plants.

Some seeds fall to the ground around the base of the plant where they will grow.

Some pods or fruits open and the seeds pop out. Sometimes, when birds eat berries, they drop the seeds.

Other seeds fall into streams, ponds, rivers or the ocean. There, they travel on the water until they stick to dirt along a shore.

The wind scatters seeds. Some seeds have
fluff on them that lets them float to the ground
like tiny parachutes. Others have wings that
spin as they fall.

Animals help scatter seeds, too. They hide
acorns and nuts in the ground. Some seeds have
hooks that stick to the fur of animals or people's
clothes. Later, they drop off onto the ground.

A flower bed or vegetable garden is beautiful!
Seeds are planted to grow in the gardens.

The seeds come in small envelopes or boxes.
Directions explain how to plant the seeds
and care for the plants.

The beginning of a plant is curled up inside each seed. Food is stored inside the seed, too. The seed has a seed coat on the outside to protect it.

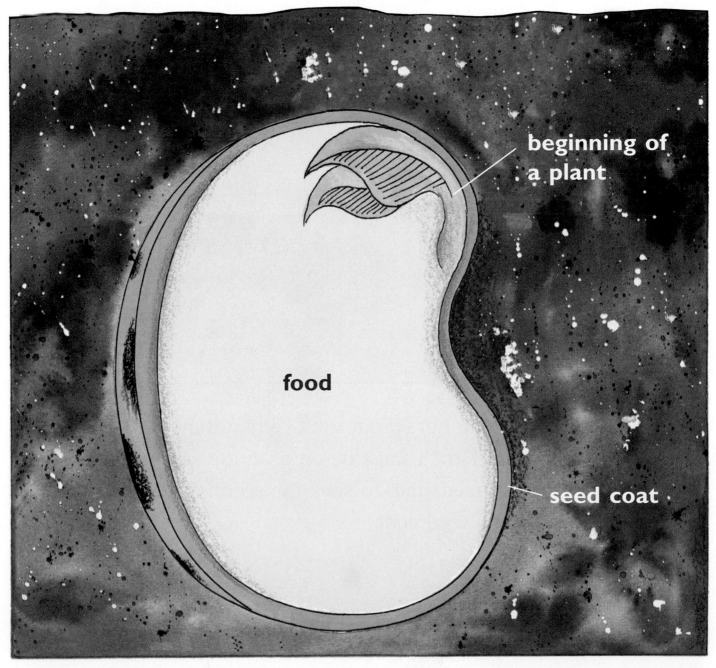

beginning of a plant

food

seed coat

A seed will not sprout until certain things
happen. First it must be on or in the soil.
Then it needs rain to soak the seed and
soften its seed coat.

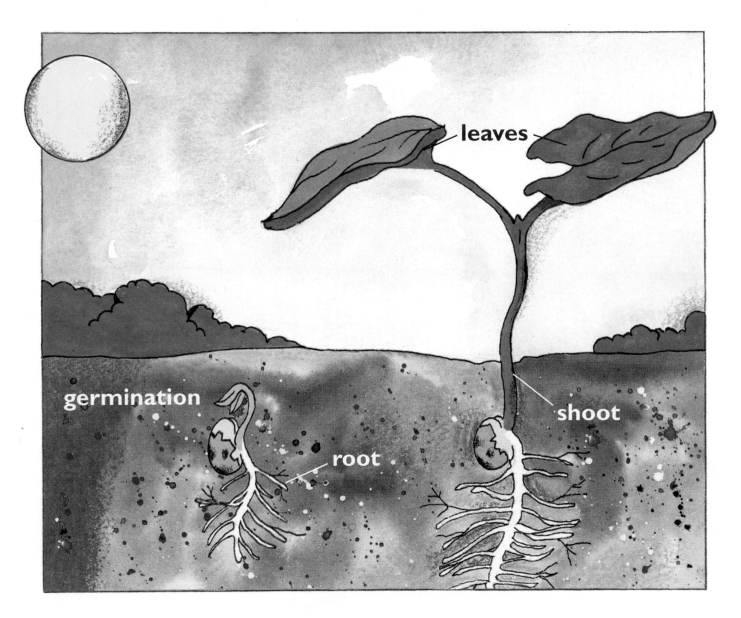

When the sun shines and warms the ground, the seed coat breaks open and the seed begins to grow. This is called germination. A root grows down into the soil. The root takes in water and minerals from the soil for food.

Up grows a shoot. Green leaves grow up from the shoot toward the sun.

The plant grows bigger and bigger. The leaves
make food for the plant from the water and
minerals in the soil, the sunlight, and the air
all around the plant.

bud

Finally, the plant is full-grown. Buds on
the plant open into flowers where new
seeds will grow.

Many of the foods people eat are seeds, fruits and pods. They are full of nutrition, vitamins and minerals and they are tasty, too!

Think and Respond

1 How does a seed become a plant?

2 Why do you think the author used diagrams to tell about the parts of a flower?

3 Why do people like to eat fruit when it **ripens**?

4 What did you learn from this story that you did not know before?

5 What strategies helped you read this selection?

Meet the Author and Illustrator
Gail Gibbons

What does Gail Gibbons need to make her books?

First, she needs ideas. She loves to write and illustrate nonfiction books. She says, "I learn a lot about the world I live in."

Next, Gail Gibbons needs time. It takes her about two months to draw all of the illustrations for one book.

What else does Gail Gibbons need? Lots of paper and plenty of paints!

Visit *The Learning Site!*
www.harcourtschool.com

A "From Seed

HOW TO RAISE BEAN PLANTS

1. Find a clean glass jar. Take a piece of black construction paper and roll it up.

2. Slide the paper into the jar. Fill the jar with water.

3. Wedge the bean seeds between the black paper and the glass. Put the jar in a warm place.

BEANS

WATCHING YOUR BEAN SEEDS WHILE THEY SPROUT

4. In a few days the seeds will begin to sprout. Watch the roots grow down. The shoots will grow up.

332

to Plant" Project

CARING FOR YOUR BEAN PLANTS

5. Put dirt into a big clay pot.

6. Carefully remove the small plants from the glass jar. Place them in the soil, covering them up to the base of their shoots.

7. Water them . . . and watch them grow!

THINK AND RESPOND

Why is it useful for people to know how plants grow?

Making Connections

Compare Texts

1. What makes "From Seed to Plant" different from "Johnny Appleseed"? Why are both selections part of the Our World theme?

2. Do you think the information in "From Seed to Plant" would be better told as a story? Why or why not?

3. How is the writing in "From Seed to Plant" and "A 'From Seed to Plant' Project" alike and different?

Write a Riddle

Write a plant riddle. Give clues that describe the plant's parts and what the plant looks like. End your riddle with "What am I?"
Have classmates guess your riddle.

Writing CONNECTION

I am a root that people eat.

I am long and orange.

What am I?

Draw a Map

lettuce
cucumbers
corn
tulips

People grow gardens all over the world. Draw a map of a garden that you would like to grow. Label the flowers, fruits, and vegetables that you would plant. Share your garden map with classmates.

Social Studies CONNECTION

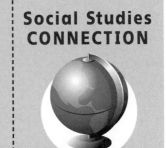

Make a Seed Packet

Choose seeds of one kind. Then design a packet for the seeds. On the front, draw a picture of what the seeds will become. On the back, write short directions for how to grow plants from the seeds.

Pumpkin Seeds

1. Plant seeds.
2. Water

Art/Science CONNECTION

335

Reading Diagrams

Focus Skill

In "From Seed to Plant," many illustrations have labels. Labeled illustrations are called **diagrams**. Diagrams show the parts of something. You can get information from a diagram.

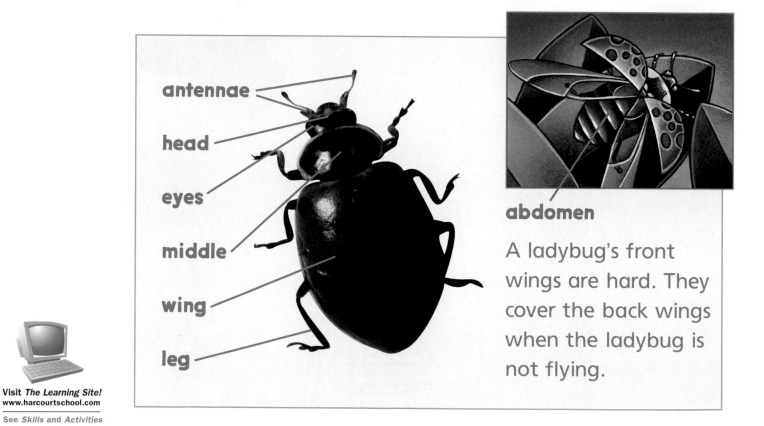

antennae
head
eyes
middle
wing
leg

abdomen

A ladybug's front wings are hard. They cover the back wings when the ladybug is not flying.

Visit *The Learning Site!*
www.harcourtschool.com

See *Skills* and *Activities*

What information does this diagram give you?

Test Prep
Reading Diagrams

Read the paragraph and the diagram. Then answer the questions.

Ladybugs

Ladybugs are insects that protect plants from other insects. Ladybugs help plants by eating the small insects that harm plants.

ladybug

aphids

1. **What does the diagram tell you?**
   - ○ the name of the insects the ladybug is eating
   - ○ the name of the plant
   - ○ how a ladybug flies

Tip
Think about the information that the labels give. Then choose your answer.

2. **Use the diagram to help you. Which of these sentences would go best at the end of the paragraph?**
   - ○ Butterflies are also insects.
   - ○ Ladybugs have two large eyes.
   - ○ These small insects are called aphids.

Tip
Choose the sentence that gives details about the main idea.

Vocabulary Power

discover

energy

forecast

shed

source

Every summer I go to a camp in the woods. I stay for a whole week.

Each morning we listen to a weather **forecast**. If the day will be rainy, we stay in and do crafts. If it will be sunny, we **shed** our sweaters. We will not put on our sweaters again until evening.

We always find new things on our walks through the woods. Sometimes we **discover** a flower that we haven't seen before. Sometimes we spot a new bird's nest.

We swim at Crystal Lake. We learn that the lake is a place where most of the animals get their food. It is also their major **source** for water.

I always go to sleep early at camp. I want to have extra **energy** the next day.

Vocabulary–Writing CONNECTION

Imagine that you are on a nature walk. Write about the plants and animals that you might **discover** along the way.

The Secret

Genre

Expository Nonfiction

Expository nonfiction explains a topic.

Look for

- **headings that tell you what each section is about.**

- **main ideas and details.**

Life of Trees

Written by Chiara Chevallier

Do you know the oldest living thing in the world?

Can you guess the heaviest living thing on Earth?

Or the tallest thing alive?

The answer to all three questions is . . . a tree!

Trees are all around us. But what do you really know about them?

Turn the page and discover the secret world of trees.

1. Tree Life

When you look at a tree, what do you see?

You see bark that protects the tree's trunk and branches. The bark at the bottom is old. It is rough and cracked. At the top the bark is young and smooth.

The tallest tree

The tallest tree alive today is over 360 feet high! It is a coast redwood growing in California. There is enough wood in its trunk to build over 300 houses!

When you look at a tree you can only see half of it!

The other half is underground.

These are the roots, pushing their way through the thick earth. They can spread out through the soil as far as the tree is high.

Rooting around

The roots of a tree that is 150 feet tall stretch under the earth for an area the size of a soccer field!

A tree can live longer than all other living things.
It can live for hundreds—even thousands—of years!

A tree needs sunlight and water to grow.

High above the ground, the tree leaves use energy from the sun to make food. Below ground, the tree's roots spread out in search of water.

The oldest tree

The oldest recorded tree in the world is a bristlecone pine. It is an amazing 4,900 years old.

When you look at a tree you can see a home for many animals and birds.

High up in the branches, birds carefully build nests. They lay their eggs out of sight and out of reach of other animals.

Under the tree branches, wasps may build a nest.

Insects and bugs live on and under a tree's bark.

Insect disguise

Some insects, like this thorn bug, disguise themselves as part of a tree so they don't get eaten.

In the earth, under the roots of a tree, rabbits and badgers dig their homes.

A tree in summer is an animal hotel!

2. Kinds of Trees

Trees come in all shapes and sizes, but there are two main types:

broad-leaved trees

and conifers.

A broad-leaved tree has large, flat leaves on its wide-spreading branches.

The shady green forests of eastern
North America are mostly made up
of broad-leaved trees.

Many broad-leaved trees change their
leaves as the seasons change.

In the cold chill of winter, most broad-leaved trees have no leaves. The leaves have dropped off because there is less sunlight.

As spring begins, fresh new leaves open from buds on the branches. The tree wakes up from its winter sleep as the days get longer and there is more sunlight.

By summer, the tree is covered with bright green leaves. The leaves give shade, shelter, and food to many animals and insects.

As the weather gets colder in the misty autumn, the tree's leaves change color. Some leaves turn brown. Others turn bright yellow or brilliant red. Then they fall to the ground. The tree is getting ready to sleep again until next spring.

Not all trees lose their leaves in winter. Some, like conifers, are evergreen.

Conifers can live in colder places than most broad-leaved trees. Instead of wide flat leaves, they have short, sharp needles that shed snow easily.

Bouncy branches

The branches of a conifer are extra bouncy. This is so they don't snap even when covered with thick snow.

Conifer trees produce hard, scaly cones to protect their seeds.

Cones come in different sizes. Some are less than half an inch. The cone of the sugar pine is two feet long.

A pine cone can help you forecast the weather! When it is warm, the scales of the cone open up.

They close again when a storm is on the way. This is to keep the seeds dry.

Wherever you are in the world you can usually find trees growing.

In steamy, wet jungles, trees grow so close together that hardly any light reaches the forest floor.

Tropical trees grow in the warmest countries of the world. Lots of tasty fruits and nuts come from tropical trees— avocados, dates, mangoes, and Brazil nuts.

Coconut palms grow wild on the beaches of many tropical countries. This palm tree's seed is inside its hairy coconut shell. The shell contains milk so the seed can start growing even if it is washed up somewhere dry.

Killer trees

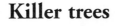

The seed of the strangler fig grows in the roots of another tree. As it grows, its roots strangle the other tree and cut out the sunlight until it dies.

When you look at a
tree you can see the
source of wood and
paper.

The table you sit at
and the chair you sit
on may be made of
wood from trees.

The swing you play
on may be made
from wood.

And the biggest secret of all? Even the book
you are reading comes from a tree!

Think and Respond

1 What interesting facts about trees did you
discover from reading this selection?

2 How does the author let you know what each box
of information is going to be about?

3 Reread pages 346 and 347. If you could give these
pages a title, what would the title be?

4 What idea in this selection would you like to learn
more about? Why?

5 What strategies helped you read this selection?
When did you use them?

Leaf Zoo

This fish is made from leaves!

Leaves come in all shapes, sizes, and colors. Do you see a long green leaf? How about a round brown leaf? Can you find a red leaf shaped like a teardrop?

How many kinds of leaves can you find in your neighborhood? Go for a walk with an adult family member and collect some. Try making your own leaf animals!

Can you name all of these leaf animals?

Making Connections

Compare Texts

(1) Think about "The Secret Life of Trees," "Johnny Appleseed," and "From Seed to Plant." How are these stories alike?

(2) Think about the writing in "Johnny Appleseed" and "From Seed to Plant." Which writing is more like "The Secret Life of Trees"? Why?

(3) How is "Leaf Zoo" different from "The Secret Life of Trees"?

A Tree Diagram

←trunk

Make a diagram to show the parts of a tree. Draw a picture of a tree, or cut a picture of a tree out of an old magazine. Attach the picture to a sheet of paper. Then label the parts, and tell what each one does.

Writing CONNECTION

Did You Use a Tree Today?

Look in your classroom for things that come from trees. Make a list of them. Think about your home. List more things that come from trees. Choose a way to share your list with classmates.

Windowsill

paper

Measure a Tree

Work with your classmates to find the distance around some tree trunks. Use a tape measure. Measure each trunk in inches and in centimeters. Record the numbers on a chart. Look at your chart to find the trees that are biggest and smallest around the trunk.

TREES AT SCHOOL

1. elm   25 in.   64 cm
2. oak   19 in.   48 cm
3. pine   33 in.   84 cm

Fact or Fiction

Focus Skill

Some books are **fiction**. They tell a story to entertain the reader. Some books tell about real things and events. They give information, or **facts**.

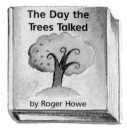

The Day the Trees Talked
by Roger Howe

This book tells a story about trees that talk to animals.

All About Pine Trees
by Claire Ramos

This book gives information, or facts, about different kinds of pine trees.

Look at the books below. Tell whether each book tells a story or gives information.

The Giant's Garden
by Mary Everly

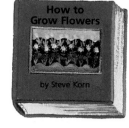

How to Grow Flowers
by Steve Korn

Tropical Plants
by Allen Weeks

The Mystery in the Woods
by Molly Summers

Visit *The Learning Site!*
www.harcourtschool.com

See Skills and Activities

Test Prep

Fact or Fiction

Look at the books below. Decide whether each book tells a story or gives facts and information. Then answer the questions.

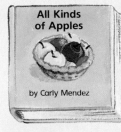

All Kinds of Apples

by Carly Mendez

Raining Blue Apples

by George Bartlett

Cooking with Apples

by Marilyn Lee

1. **Which book would you use to find out how to make an apple pie?**

   ○ All Kinds of Apples

   ○ Raining Blue Apples

   ○ Cooking with Apples

2. **Which book probably tells a story?**

   ○ All Kinds of Apples

   ○ Raining Blue Apples

   ○ Cooking with Apples

Tip

Use what you know about fact and fiction to choose the best answer.

Vocabulary Power

beneath

knelt

relay race

shimmered

snug

wrinkled

Hi! This is me — Maria! I took these pictures of my family last summer.

Grandmother sat **beneath** the oak tree. Doesn't she look **snug** and comfortable? Mom **knelt** beside her.

My brothers and cousins ran in a **relay race**.

My brother **wrinkled** his face to look just like our dog's face!

When it got hot, we jumped into the pool. The water **shimmered** and sparkled in the sun.

Vocabulary–Writing CONNECTION

Draw a picture of something you did last summer. Write a caption for it. Use one or more Vocabulary Power words in your caption.

Genre

Realistic Fiction

Realistic fiction tells about characters that are like people in real life.

Look for

- **characters that have feelings that real people have.**
- **a setting that could be a real place.**

WATER

by Kathi Appelt

MELON DAY

illustrated by Dale Gottlieb

That watermelon grew in the corner of the patch where the fence posts met. Jesse found it early one day while pulling weeds. It was not as big as her fist, but it was bigger than the other melons still hiding beneath their mamas' fuzzy leaves.

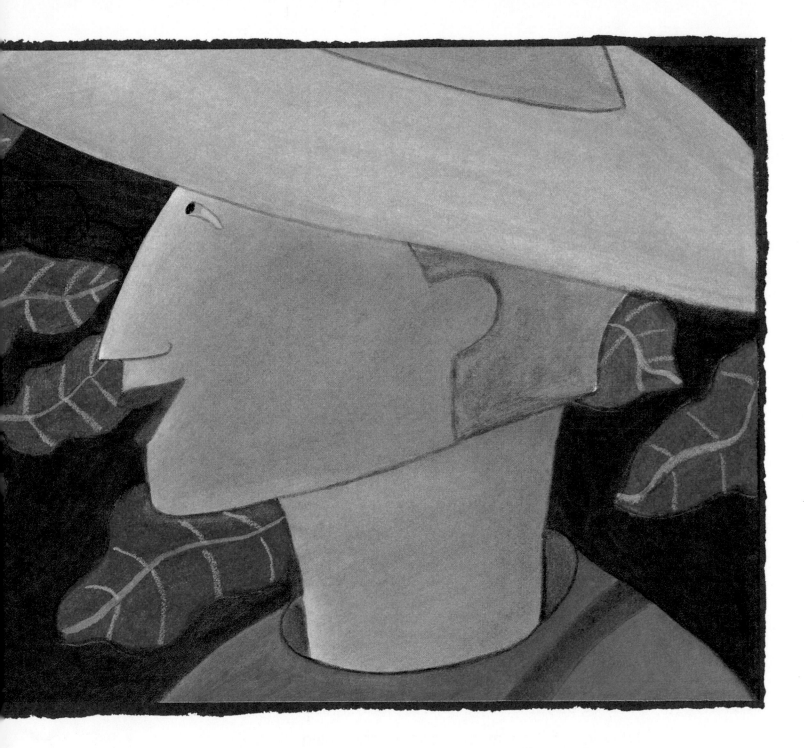

When she showed it to Pappy, he smiled. "Yep, it'll be a big one all right. It'll be just right for a Watermelon Day."

"A Watermelon Day!"

Jesse knew what that meant. There would be cousins, big and small. Mama's peach ice cream. Innings and innings of softball. Relay races and apple-bobbing. Uncle Ike with his banjo. Finally, to top it all, ice-cold watermelon—the biggest one from the patch.

Thinking about it made Jesse's mouth water.

"How long till it's ready, Pappy?" she asked.

"Got a whole summer to go yet," he answered.

Jesse looked at the small melon. It was round and snug in the sand. She smiled.

Every day Jesse walked up and down the rows of the patch. When she got to her melon, she knelt beside it and put her ear against its dark green rind.

She patted it with her palm. At first it made a thick, dull sound, like Pappy's boots when he dropped them on the front porch. But as the days passed, the sound grew brighter. Jesse patted the other melons, too. Some sounded dull. Some sounded bright. But hers had the sweetest song.

"How much longer, Pappy?" she asked.
"Not much longer now," he answered.

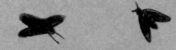

The summer days grew longer. Jesse's watermelon got riper. Its stripes began to zig and zag.

Jesse waited. She waited until the days were so hot she had to wear shoes so her feet wouldn't blister in the sand. So hot the air wrinkled up like an unironed shirt. So hot that hardly anything moved except the flies.

She waited until she thought she and her watermelon might both burst from the sheer waiting of it all.

One morning, when the relatives were coming, Jesse asked, "How much longer, Pappy?" Pappy looked at Jesse. He looked at the watermelon patch. He looked at the blue summer sky. "Well," he answered, "this looks like a Watermelon Day."

"A Watermelon Day!"

Jesse skipped to the corner of the patch where the fence posts met. She patted her watermelon. It was full of the cool summer rains. Full of the warmth from its sandy nest. Full of the deep hot sun.

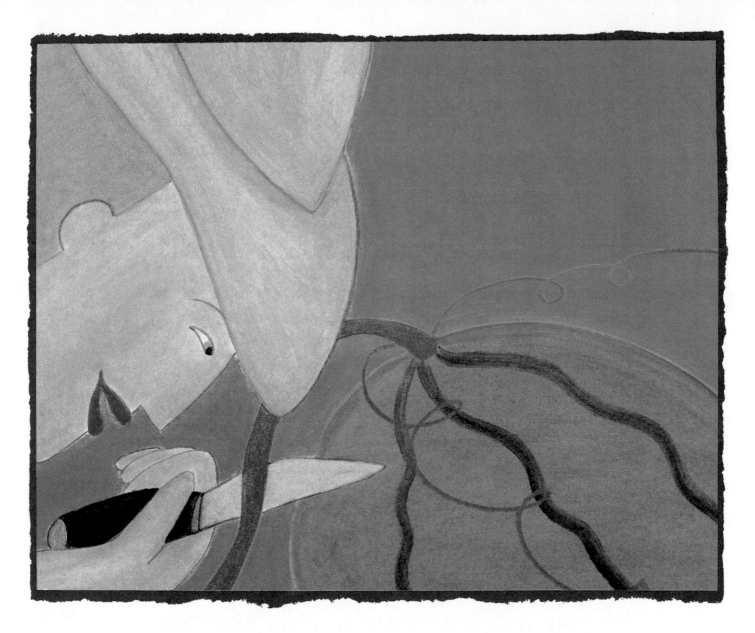

Pappy cut the ropelike vine with his pocketknife and carried the melon out of the patch, past the front porch and down to the lake. He set it in the cold, cold water. There it floated, right along the edge, beneath the deep blue shade of the weeping willow tree.

"How long will it take, Pappy?" asked Jesse.

"Most of the day," he answered. "There's a whole summer's worth of heat inside it."

Jesse's watermelon floated all that hot day long.
Willow branches dipped up and down, testing the icy
water. That melon floated while the cousins came.

It floated while Mama dished out peach ice cream.

It floated through a game of softball and several relay races.

It even floated while Uncle Ike played "Turkey in the Straw."

And all the while Jesse thought about it, her mouth watered.

Watermelon, watermelon.

"How much longer, Pappy?" she asked.
"Oh, it's not ready yet," he answered.

The day stretched and stretched like a lazy ol' cat. Jesse waited and waited.

She waited through more innings of softball. She waited through apple-bobbing. She waited through freeze-tag. She waited through Uncle Ike's rendition of "Stars and Stripes Forever."

At last the sun began to sink. The sweat dried on Jesse's neck. The lake shimmered. "How much longer, Pappy?" she asked. Pappy looked at Jesse. He looked at the sinking sun. He looked at the shimmery lake. "I think it's good and cold now," he answered.

Jesse hopped. She skipped. She danced all the way to the lake. Pappy lifted the melon out of the icy water and carried it to the front porch, where he set it down.

With the side of his fist, Pappy hit that melon right in the deep, deep middle.

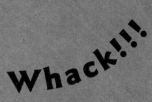

Whack!!!

Craaack!!!

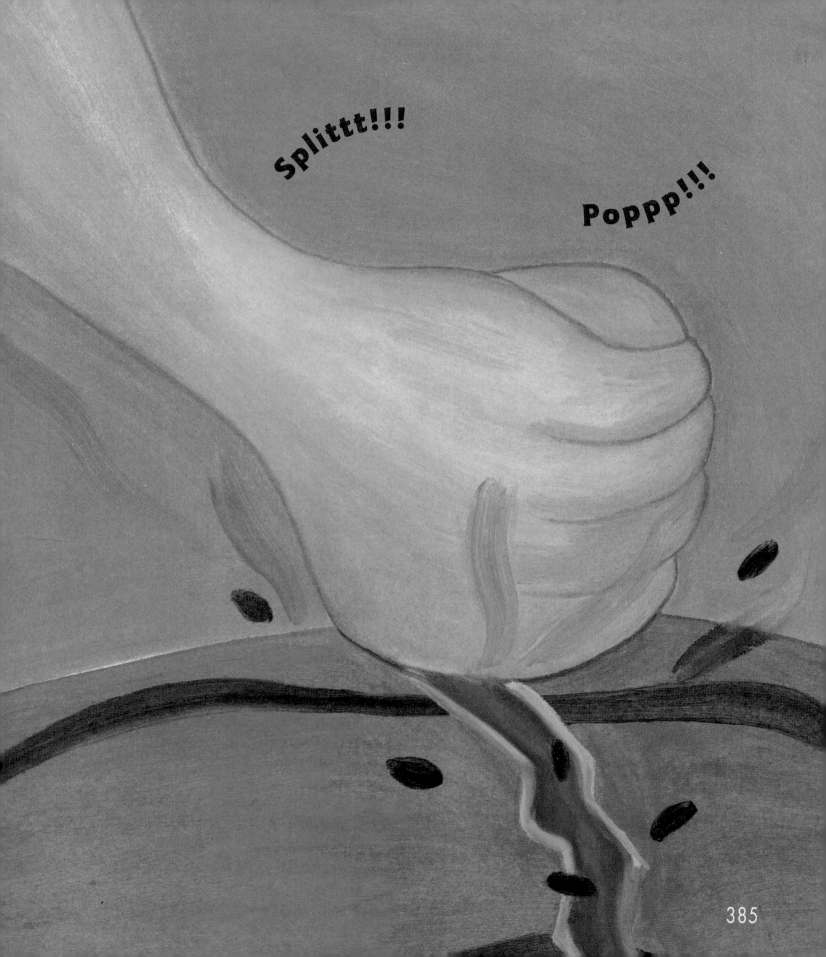

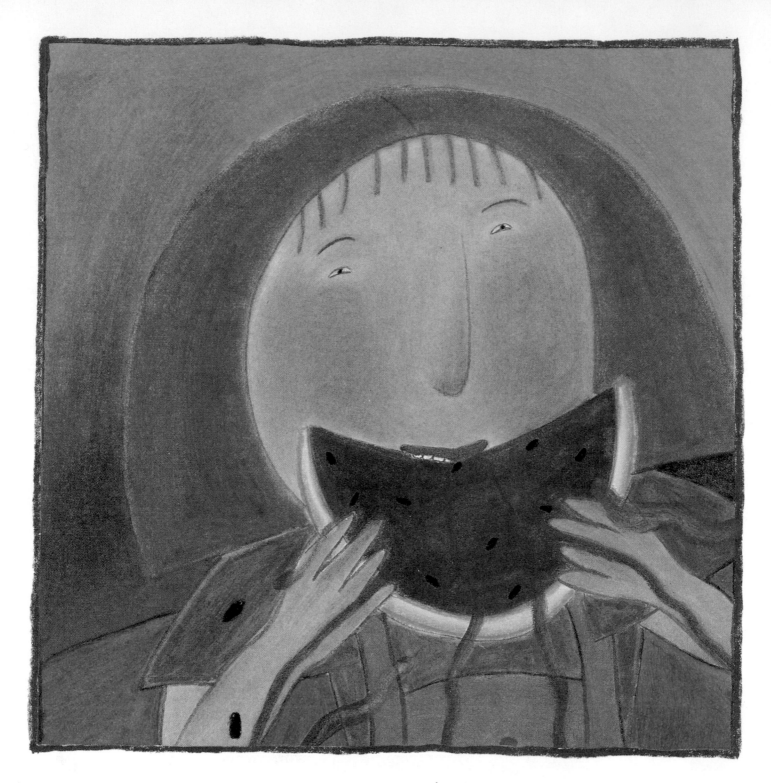

Red, red juice ran down Jesse's chin. It ran down
her hand and between her fingers. It splashed onto
her toes.

That melon was sweet. Sweet as the summer rain.
Sweet as a nighttime song. That melon was cold. Cold as
a puppy's nose. Cold as the deep blue lake.

Jesse smiled. She danced. She spit watermelon seeds
into the sky. She sang a watermelon song.

Watermelon, watermelon.

It's a Watermelon Day!

Think and Respond

1. How does Jesse feel about her watermelon?

2. Why do you think the author says the air **wrinkled** up like an unironed shirt?

3. How does Jesse's watermelon help her understand nature?

4. What would you like to grow in a garden? Why?

5. Which strategies helped you read this story?

Meet the Author and the Illustrator

Kathi Appelt

Would your mother be upset if you drew on the walls? Kathi Appelt's mother wasn't. Kathi and her sisters drew pictures on the walls of their garage. Later, Kathi wrote poetry on the walls, too. She now lives in Texas with her family and writes children's books. But Kathi Appelt doesn't write on walls anymore. Now she uses a computer.

Dale Gottlieb

Besides illustrating children's books, Dale Gottlieb makes what she calls "story rugs." The pictures in the rugs tell stories. She gets ideas for her rugs from stories she reads and even the children's stories she writes. You can see her rugs in Seattle, Washington.

Visit *The Learning Site!*
www.harcourtschool.com

389

Making Connections

Compare Texts

1. Why do you think "Watermelon Day" is part of a theme called Our World?

2. How is the main character in "Watermelon Day" like and different from the main character in "Johnny Appleseed"?

3. How is "Watermelon Day" written differently from "From Seed to Plant"? Which gives more information?

Watermelon Day Invitation

August 25, 2003

Dear Terry,
    Please come to my Watermelon Day party at noon on Saturday, September 5. I live at 25 Oak Lane. We will play lots of games.

Your friend,
Clarisa

Write a letter inviting friends to your own Watermelon Day party. Include the five parts of a letter.

Writing
CONNECTION

Map It Out

Where do watermelons grow best in the United States? Why? Find out and make a map that shows the states where most watermelons are grown. Share your information.

Social Studies
CONNECTION

Social Studies
CONNECTION

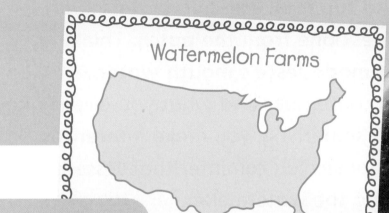

Watermelon Farms

Share a Melon

How could you share a watermelon so that each of your classmates gets a piece about the same size? Make a plan to show how the class could cut up one large melon. Present your plan. Use drawings to help you.

Math
CONNECTION

Make Inferences

Focus Skill

Read these sentences from "Watermelon Day". What does it mean to say that Jesse's mouth waters?

Finally, to top it all, ice-cold watermelon— the biggest one from the patch. Thinking about it made Jesse's mouth water.

When you use clues and what you already know to understand something, you **make inferences**. From the sentences above, you can infer that Jesse is thinking about eating the watermelon.

This chart shows how you might make inferences as you read "Watermelon Day."

Clues from Story +	What We Know =	Inference
Jesse's watermelon is the biggest in the patch.	Pappy says it will be just right for a Watermelon Day.	The biggest watermelon in the patch is the best for a Watermelon Day.
Jesse is excited about the watermelon.	People eat watermelons.	

What inference might you write in the last box?

Test Prep
Make Inferences

Read the paragraph. Then answer the questions.

Olivia's World

Olivia woke up with the sun shining in her eyes. She looked around the room. Her little sister was asleep in the next bed. There were boxes everywhere. Then she heard her father's voice. "Wake up, girls! Time to see the new neighborhood."

---

1. **It is most likely that —**
   - ○ Olivia is lost
   - ○ Olivia is staying with a friend
   - ○ Olivia's family has moved
   - ○ Olivia is having a dream

Tip

Reread the paragraph to make sure you have the important information.

2. **This story most likely takes place —**
   - ○ late at night
   - ○ in the morning
   - ○ late in the afternoon
   - ○ right after dinner

Tip

Use word clues and what you already know to make inferences about a story.

Vocabulary Power

▲ Pumpkin Fiesta

boasted
crept
crown
village
vines

I live in Bolton, a small **village** with farms around it. Last fall we had a harvest parade.

Each farmer made a float for the parade. One float had pumpkins still on their curly, green **vines**. A funny scarecrow grinned at us as the float **crept** slowly along.

My older sister, Ella, was chosen to be Harvest Queen. She wore a **crown** on her head and waved to all the people.

Ella **boasted** about being Harvest Queen for a week. Every morning she would put on her crown and remind me that she had won. I was happy for her, so I didn't mind too much!

Vocabulary-Writing CONNECTION

Imagine that you could give a **crown** to someone to wear. Who would you give it to, and why? Write a paragraph that explains your ideas.

Pump

Story

A story has characters, a setting, and a plot.

Look for

- a plot with a beginning, a middle, and an end.

- pictures that help tell the story.

kin Fiesta

by Caryn Yacowitz
illustrated by Joe Cepeda

Old Juana grew the biggest, roundest, and orangest pumpkins in the whole province of San Miguel. For as long as anyone could remember, she had won the special pumpkin crown at the big fiesta each year.

Everyone in her village was proud of Old Juana.
All except her neighbor, Foolish Fernando.

"I will discover Old Juana's secret, and this year
my pumpkins will be the finest at the *fiesta*,"
Fernando boasted to his pet bull, Toro.

At planting time Fernando followed Old Juana to Pumpkin Hill and hid behind a bush. He watched as Juana and her little burro, Dulcita, plowed the field. Old Juana broke up the clods of soil with her hoe until they crumbled like fresh cake in her hands.

Her faded cotton dress fluttered in the cool spring breeze. Her big straw hat cast a pool of shadow on the freshly tilled soil. Old Juana bent so low that her chin almost touched her knees as she carefully planted plump, white pumpkin seeds—one, two, three to a mound.

Foolish Fernando watched and watched.
Then he ran home as fast as his skinny legs
could carry him.

Early the next day Fernando began hoeing his plot of land. He wore a faded cotton dress and a big straw hat. He quickly scattered seeds in every direction.

"I looked just like Old Juana today," Foolish Fernando said, scratching Toro behind the ears. "I'm sure that is the secret to her pumpkins."

Soon the warm spring rains came. The vines on Old Juana's Pumpkin Hill grew strong. Their twisting tendrils hugged the ground.

Fernando looked at his scrawny vines. Could there be another secret? he wondered.

The next morning when Old Juana and Dulcita passed by, carrying heavy jugs of water from the well, Fernando left his favorite spot in the pepper tree and followed them to Pumpkin Hill.

"*Agua, agua.* Water, water, my beauties." Old Juana's words carried on the warm wind as she gave each plant a cool drink. "Butter babies, butter babies," she cooed to each yellow blossom. "Open your faces to the sun, invite the honey bees to visit you. Soon you will grow to be fat, round pumpkins."

"*¡Si! ¡Si!* Yes! Yes!" Fernando cried. When he got home, he put on the faded cotton dress and his straw hat. Fernando scooped some water into an old clay pot. He ran back to Pumpkin Hill.

"*Agua, agua,*" he called. "Water, water, my beauties." He splashed a few drops of water on his plants. "Baby butters, butter balls, buttercups." A drop of water landed here, another splashed there. "Big butters, baby cups, butter-ups," Fernando said. He talked to his pumpkins until the sun set.

Before he went to bed, Fernando danced a little jig. "I know the secret of Pumpkin Hill," he told Toro. "I looked like Old Juana and talked like her, too! I will wear the pumpkin crown this year!"

407

All the long, hot summer Old Juana and Dulcita carried water to Pumpkin Hill. The yellow blossoms turned into baby pumpkins. A few grew to be as large and as round as wagon wheels. Old Juana named her three finest pumpkins Gorda, who was the chubbiest, Linda, the prettiest, and Blush Bottom, for her color.

Fernando talked to his plants, but he often forgot to water them.

Only a few blossoms turned into small, green pumpkins. "Something is not right," he said. "I will watch Old Juana one last time."

Fernando ran to Pumpkin Hill and hid. He watched as Old Juana and Dulcita carefully picked insects off the vines.

"*¡Por supuesto!* Of course!" he cried. "Why didn't I see it before? Toro will have to help me."

The next morning Fernando gathered straw and twine. He went to his field, pulling Toro behind him.

Foolish Fernando plucked one hungry bug from one leaf. Toro stood near him, embarrassed; his head hung low.

"Well done," declared Fernando that evening. "I know all the secrets now. I looked and talked just like Old Juana, and you, my precious pet, looked just like Dulcita! I'm sure my pumpkins will be the finest at the *fiesta!*"

But Toro charged away to the farthest corner of the field and did not come back, even at midnight.

By autumn Old Juana's biggest pumpkins—
Gorda, Linda, and Blush Bottom—had all turned
the color of the harvest moon.

Fernando's pumpkins were small, shriveled,
and green.

The night before the *fiesta* Fernando crept
among the vines of Pumpkin Hill. With a whack
and a chop he cut Gorda, Linda, and Blush Bottom
from their vines and heaved them into his cart.

At dawn on *fiesta* day Old Juana and Dulcita arrived at Pumpkin Hill. Old Juana looked at the spot where her beautiful pumpkins had grown. She could not believe her eyes. "Where are my children?" she cried. "Who has stolen my beauties?"

She searched every corner of Pumpkin Hill.

When she was sure they were nowhere to be found, Old Juana took a knife and bent over the vines where Gorda, Linda, and Blush Bottom had grown.

With heavy hearts Old Juana and Dulcita traveled the dusty road to the *fiesta*.

When they arrived, they heard music and cheering. Pushing through the crowd, Old Juana spied Gorda, Linda, and Blush Bottom. There, sitting proudly behind them, grinned Foolish Fernando! The mayor held the pumpkin crown over Fernando's head.

"Stop! Stop!" Old Juana cried. The music ceased. The crowd was silent. All eyes were on Old Juana.

414

"Those are my pumpkins!" she cried. A look of shock spread through the crowd.

"What proof do you have that these are your pumpkins?" asked the mayor.

"I tilled the soil and planted the seeds on Pumpkin Hill. I carried water to the plants every day. I removed the insects that ate the leaves," Juana replied.

"Perhaps so," said the mayor, "but you must show us proof."

"The pumpkins are mine," said Juana. "I can prove it." She reached deep into her pocket and pulled out the stubs of the vines where each pumpkin had been cut. "Here is Gorda's. And Linda's—see how it fits her like a little cap. And this one belongs to my precious Blush Bottom."

A murmur swept the crowd. "These are indeed Old Juana's pumpkins!" shouted the mayor. He placed the crown on Old Juana's head.

The crowd let out a roar.

"*¡Viva Juana! ¡Viva Juana!*" they chanted. "Long live Juana! Long live Juana!"

417

Foolish Fernando was about to sneak away when the mayor scooped him up and brought him to Old Juana.

Fernando stood before her, his head bent low.

"I'm sorry, Juana," said Fernando. "I was wrong to take your pumpkins."

"Foolish, Foolish Fernando," said Old Juana. "Do you really want to grow beautiful, big pumpkins?"

"*¡Si!¡Si!*" shouted Fernando.

"Will you pay attention and do as I say?" asked Old Juana.

"*¡Si! ¡Si! ¡Te prometo!* Yes! Yes! I promise you!" shouted Fernando.

"Well," said Old Juana with a smile, "then I will teach you."

And Old Juana taught Foolish Fernando the secret of Pumpkin Hill.

Think and Respond

1. What does Foolish Fernando do to try to win the pumpkin **crown**?

2. How do the author and illustrator make this story funny?

3. What is the secret of Pumpkin Hill?

4. What is your favorite part of the story? Why?

5. Which strategies did you use to help you read this story? Why?

Meet the Author

Caryn Yacowitz

Caryn Yacowitz loves to garden. She and her family once grew a 53-pound pumpkin! They later turned it into a big soup bowl. What kind of soup did they serve? Pumpkin soup, of course!

Caryn Yacowitz and her family live in Palo Alto, California.

Meet the Illustrator
Joe Cepeda

Like Foolish Fernando, Joe Cepeda loves pumpkins. His wife says that he can eat a whole pumpkin pie by himself at Thanksgiving! When he's not illustrating picture books, he likes to make things out of wood.

Joe Cepeda lives with his family in Rosemead, California.

Making Connections

Compare Texts

1   Why do you think "Pumpkin Fiesta" is in a theme called Our World?

2   How is Foolish Fernando different from Johnny Appleseed?

3   In what ways are the stories "Watermelon Day" and "Pumpkin Fiesta" alike?

How to Grow a Pumpkin

Think about how Old Juana made her pumpkins grow big and round. Write steps for growing pumpkins. Use events from the story to help you. Make sure your steps are in order.

How to Grow a Pumpkin
1. Plow the field.
2.

Writing CONNECTION

422

Fruits of Science

Did you know that a pumpkin is actually a fruit? Pumpkins are the fruit of pumpkin plants. A pumpkin has seeds inside to help it grow new plants. Make a list of fruits with seeds inside. Make sure to include:

- a fruit with a peel
- a fruit that is not sweet
- a fruit that grows on trees
- a green fruit
- your favorite fruit

All About Mexico

This story takes place in Mexico. Find Mexico on a map. Is Mexico north or south of the United States? Is it bigger or smaller than the United States? What oceans are next to it? Talk with classmates about what you find out.

Adding -s and -es to Words

When you want to change a noun that names one thing to a noun that names more than one thing, add **-s** or **-es** to a word.

> **one pumpkin → two pumpkins**

Use these rules to add **-s** or **-es** to words.

- Add just **-s** to most words.

  garden → gardens   vine → vines

- Add **-es** to words that end in **sh**, **ch**, **x**, **s**, or **z**.

  wish → wishes   buzz → buzzes

- If a word ends with a consonant and **y**, change the **y** to **i** and add **-es**.

  baby → babies   try → tries

Use these tips to add -s or -es.

- Add just **-s** to most words.
- Add **-es** to words that end in **sh**, **ch**, **x**, **s**, or **z**.
- If a word ends with a consonant and **y**, change the **y** to **i** and add **-es**.

Test Prep

Adding -s and -es to Words

Fill in the bubble next to the word that is spelled correctly.

Example: **ferry**

○ ferrys

○ ferryes

● ferries

1.   **bring**

○ brings

○ bringes

○ bringies

2.   **army**

○ armies

○ armeys

○ armys

3.   **crash**

○ crashs

○ crashies

○ crashes

Tip

Look at the letter before the *y*. Think about the rule for words that end in *y*.

Tip

Say each choice aloud. Which sounds best?

Writer's Handbook

Contents

Purposes for Writing

There are many different **purposes for writing.**
People may write to give information, to entertain, to
give an opinion, or to express ideas.

Some Purposes for Writing	Examples
to give information	• how-to paragraph • research report
to entertain	• funny story • poem
to give an opinion	• poster that persuades • book review
to express ideas	• journal entry • letter

Try This

What would be the purpose for writing a paragraph about
kinds of cats?

The Writing Process

When you write, use a plan to help you. Think about *what* you want to write, for *whom* you are writing, and *why* you are writing. Then use these stages to help you as you write.

Revise

Read what you have written. Add important ideas and details that you left out. Be sure your information is in an order that makes sense.

Draft

Write your ideas in sentences and paragraphs. Do not worry about making mistakes.

Prewrite

Plan what you will write. Choose your topic, and organize your information.

Proofread

Check for errors. Correct mistakes in capital letters, end marks, and spelling.

Publish

Choose a way to share your writing. You can add pictures, graphs, or charts.

Try This

In your journal, list the five writing stages. Draw a picture with five parts like the one above to help you remember each stage.

How to Get Ideas

Writers find **topics,** or ideas, for writing in many ways. One way is to **brainstorm** ideas. When you brainstorm, you make a list of all the ideas that come to your mind. This is a list of ideas for a story about places to play.

Where I Like to Play

backyard

park

my bedroom

Writers also brainstorm ideas by using a **word web.**

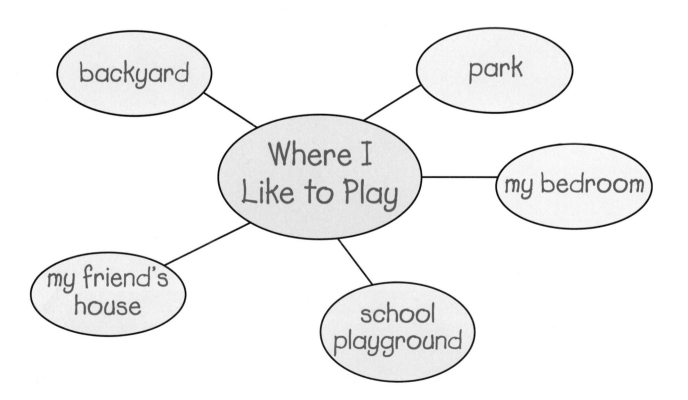

Writers ask **questions** to get ideas for their writing. They write a few questions and then find the answers before they begin writing. These questions are for a research report about trucks.

Trucks That Help Us

What kinds of trucks help people do jobs?

What do these trucks do?

Another way to get ideas is to write in your **journal.** You can keep a record of interesting things that happen to write about later.

September 2, 2003

Today was my first piano lesson. I was so nervous, but I loved playing! The half hour flew by. My teacher said I did a great job.

Try This

Choose an animal that you would like to write about. Brainstorm a list of words that tell about it.

431

Dictionary

A **dictionary** is a book that gives the meanings of words. It may also give an example sentence that shows how to use the word. A **synonym,** or word that has the same meaning, may come after the example sentence. The **entry words** are in ABC order, or alphabetical order. If a word has more than one meaning, each meaning has a number.

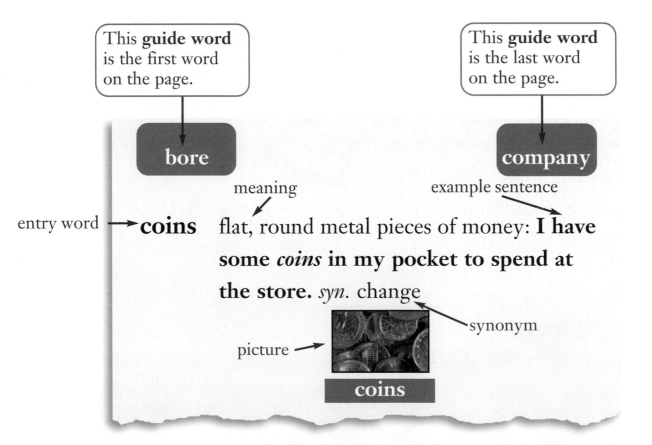

This **guide word** is the first word on the page.

This **guide word** is the last word on the page.

bore

company

meaning

example sentence

entry word → **coins** flat, round metal pieces of money: **I have some *coins* in my pocket to spend at the store.** *syn.* change

synonym

picture →

coins

Thesaurus

A **thesaurus** is a list of words and their synonyms. Sometimes a thesaurus lists antonyms, too. An **antonym** is a word that has the opposite meaning. A good time to use a thesaurus is when you are looking for a more interesting word or a more exact word.

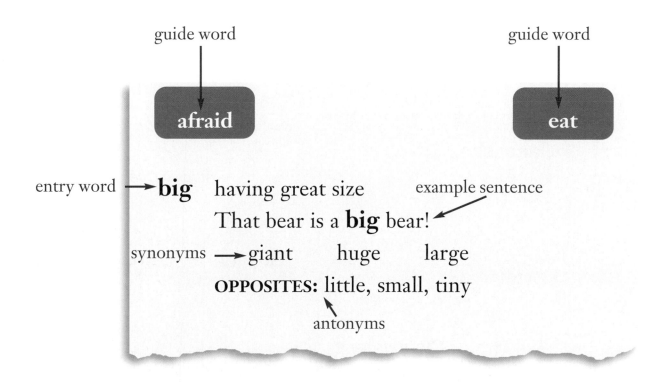

guide word

afraid

guide word

eat

entry word ⟶ **big** having great size

example sentence

That bear is a **big** bear!

synonyms ⟶ giant   huge   large

OPPOSITES: little, small, tiny

antonyms

Try This

Choose a word. Look it up in the dictionary and in the thesaurus. What do you find that is the same in both books? What is different?

Atlas

An **atlas** is a book of maps. An atlas of the United States has maps of all the states. The maps show cities, bodies of waters, and mountains. Sometimes the maps show where products are made. Look in an atlas's Table of Contents or Index to find the map you need.

Map of Florida

Newspaper

A **newspaper** gives the news. It can tell what is happening around the world and in your town.

A newspaper tells about many subjects. It can tell about neighborhood events, sports, art, business, and the weather. Newspaper articles tell *who, what, where, when, why,* and *how.*

Magazine

A **magazine** gives information in stories and pictures. Magazines usually come out once a week or once a month.

Magazines can be about one main subject, such as science, skating, baseball, or doll collecting. Some magazines are written for certain groups of people, such as children, parents, or older people.

Try This

Find a newspaper article about a place. Find the place in an atlas. What does the atlas tell about it?

Parts of a Book

Most books have special pages that give information about what is inside. The **table of contents,** in the front, shows the chapters of a book. It also gives the page number for the beginning of each chapter.

A **glossary,** at the back, tells the meanings of important words in the book.

Table of Contents

An **index,** also at the back, lists the subjects in the book. The subjects are in alphabetical order. The index gives the page numbers where you can find those subjects.

Index

Using a Computer

A computer can help you in many ways as you write. You can use **spell-check** to find and correct words that are misspelled.

Spell-Check

Word to Check: spel

replace

cancel

spell
spill
sped

You can use a computer's **search engine** to find information. A **key word** tells what your topic is. Type a key word and click on *Go*.

Search by Word

Go

Search for: dinosaurs

You can also use a computer to get and send e-mail messages. To send e-mail, you need a person's e-mail address.

Try This

Find a book about your favorite sport. Look at the table of contents. Choose a chapter that interests you and read some of it. Then use a word-processing program to write a short paragraph about what you read.

Story

A story has a beginning, a middle, and an end. A good story has strong characters, a setting, and a problem to solve.

A **story map** is a chart that shows the parts of a story. Writers use story maps to plan their stories during the prewriting stage. A writer answers the questions in each part of the story map.

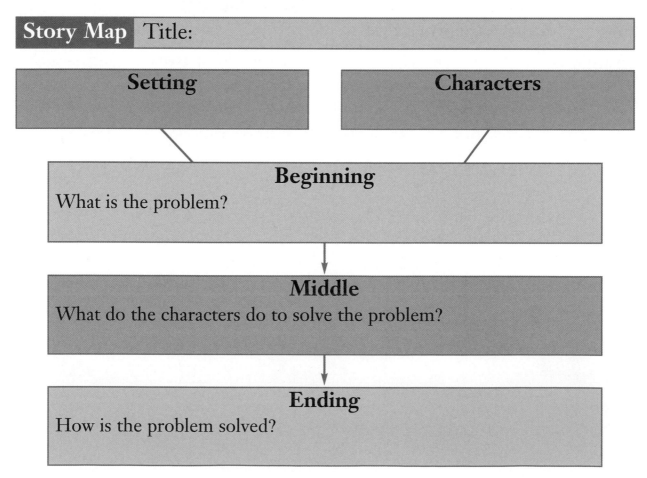

Story Map	Title:

Setting

Characters

Beginning
What is the problem?

Middle
What do the characters do to solve the problem?

Ending
How is the problem solved?

A **sequence chart** is another way to organize a story. Writers often use sequence charts to write personal stories. In a **personal story,** a writer tells about something that happened in his or her life.

In a sequence chart, the writer answers questions about what happens **first, next,** and **last** in a personal story.

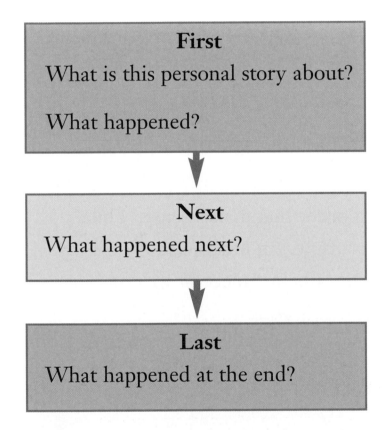

First

What is this personal story about?

What happened?

Next

What happened next?

Last

What happened at the end?

Try This

Think about a story you know. Make a story map to show the parts of the story.

Report: Note Taking

In a **research report,** a writer gives information about a topic. To find information for a report, you can write questions on **note cards.** Then search on a computer and at the library to find the answers. Write the answers on your note cards.

When did dinosaurs live?

- The last dinosaur died about 65 million years ago.
- The first dinosaur lived about 245 million years ago.
- No one knows for sure why they died.

Put your note cards in an order that makes sense. Then use the cards to write an outline. An **outline** shows the order of **main ideas** and **details** in a piece of writing.

Dinosaurs Outline

1. When did Dinosaurs live?
   a. last dinosaur, 65 million years ago
   b. first dinosaur, 245 million years ago
   c. No one knows why they died.
2. What kinds of dinosaurs were there?
   a. Tyrannosaurus rex
   b. Stegosaurus
   c. Troodon

Use your outline to organize your report. The questions become the **main ideas.** Write a paragraph about each main idea. The answers you found are the **details** about the main ideas.

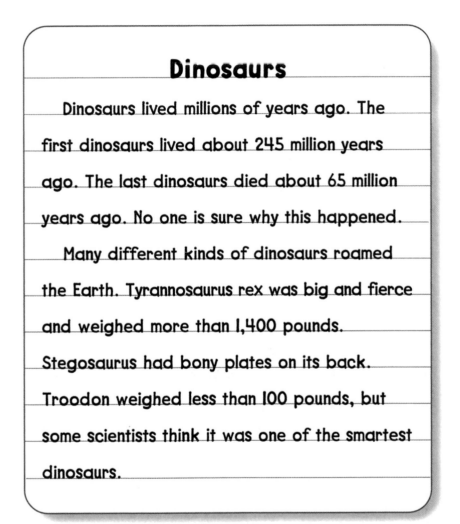

Dinosaurs

Dinosaurs lived millions of years ago. The first dinosaurs lived about 245 million years ago. The last dinosaurs died about 65 million years ago. No one is sure why this happened.

Many different kinds of dinosaurs roamed the Earth. Tyrannosaurus rex was big and fierce and weighed more than 1,400 pounds. Stegosaurus had bony plates on its back. Troodon weighed less than 100 pounds, but some scientists think it was one of the smartest dinosaurs.

Try This

Think about what you do on a weekend morning. Take notes about what you do, and write an outline.

Traits of Good Writing

All good writers ask themselves questions like these about what they write.

Focus/Ideas

- Is my message clear and interesting?
- Do I have enough information?

Organization

- Do I have a good beginning and a good ending?
- Is my information or my story in the right order?

Development

- Do each of my paragraphs have a main idea?
- Do I include important details in my paragraphs?

Voice

- Do I sound like myself?
- Do I say in an interesting way what I think or feel?

Word Choice

- Do my words make sense?
- Do I use interesting words?

Sentences

- Do I begin my sentences in different ways?
- Does my writing sound smooth when I read it aloud?

Conventions

- Do I indent my paragraphs?
- Are my spelling, punctuation marks, and capital letters correct?

Writers use **editor's marks** like these as they **revise** and **proofread** their writing.

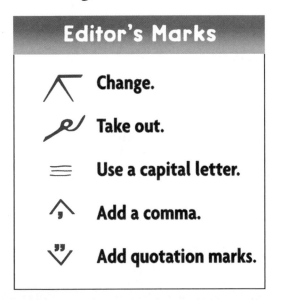

Editor's Marks

⅄	Change.
ℓ	Take out.
≡	Use a capital letter.
⌃,	Add a comma.
⌄"	Add quotation marks.

Try This

Read a story with a partner. Talk about the traits of good writing that you find in the story.

Using a Rubric

A **rubric** is a checklist you can use to make your writing better. Here is how you can use a rubric.

Before writing Look at the checklist to find out what your piece of writing should have.

During writing Check your draft against the list. Use the list to see how to make your writing better.

After writing Check your finished work against the list. Does your work show all the points?

Your Best Score

✔ Your writing is focused.

✔ You write about your ideas in an order that makes sense.

✔ You give important details about the main idea.

✔ Your writing sounds like you.

✔ You use words that are clear.

✔ Your sentences begin differently and fit together well.

✔ Your writing has few or no mistakes in punctuation, capitalization, or grammar.

Peer Conferences

After you have written your first draft, you are ready to revise your writing. A class partner can help. Follow these steps to have a peer conference. A **peer conference** is a meeting with a partner or small group to help you make your writing better.

Revising Your Writing

1. Read your first draft aloud. Then let your partner read it silently.

2. Talk with your partner about ways to make your draft better.

3. Take notes about changes you need to make.

Revising Your Partner's Writing

1. Listen carefully to your partner's draft read aloud. Then read it slowly yourself.

2. Tell two or three things that you like about it.

3. Give your partner one or two suggestions for making the draft better.

Try This

Meet with a partner to talk about your writing. Together, go over the traits of good writing. Talk about the traits your writing has.

Handwriting Tips

It is important to write neatly and clearly so that others can read your writing. Follow these handwriting tips.

- Hold your pencil and place your paper as shown.

left hand

right hand

- Sit up straight. Face your desk, and place both feet on the floor.

- Make your letters smooth and even.

- Make sure your letters are not too close together or too far apart.

correct	too close	too far apart

- Begin writing to the right of the red line on your paper. Leave a space as wide as a pencil.

- The space between words or between sentences should be as wide as a pencil.

- Make sure tall letters touch the top line, short letters touch the midline, and the tails of letters hang below the base line.

Try This

Use your best handwriting to write a letter to a friend.

Using Computer Graphics

You can use your computer to add graphics, or pieces of art, to your writing.

- **Use different kinds of type.** Using different kinds of type and different colors makes writing fun to read.

- **Add pictures to a story.** Use pictures from your word processing program, or use a separate drawing program. Add art to your story to make a book.

- **Add frames and borders.**

- **Add charts or graphs to a report.** Use your computer to make charts and graphs. Show them as you share your report with your classmates.

Pictograph

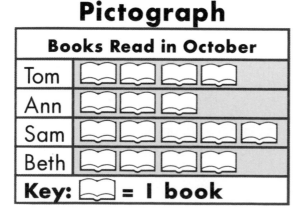

Bar Graph

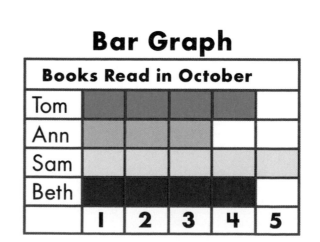

Oral Presentations

You may want to give an **oral presentation** of your writing. Here are some ways to keep your listeners interested.

- Plan your presentation. Decide how you will read or present your writing.

- Hold your paper low so that listeners can see your face.

- Look at your listeners when you speak.

- Use your voice to show funny, sad, or exciting parts of your writing.

- Speak loudly and clearly so that everyone can hear you.

- Use drawings, charts, or time lines to help make your writing interesting and clear.

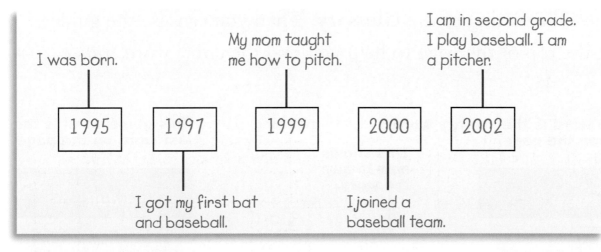

I was born. — **1995**

I got my first bat and baseball. — **1997**

My mom taught me how to pitch. — **1999**

I joined a baseball team. — **2000**

I am in second grade. I play baseball. I am a pitcher. — **2002**

Try This

Think about something exciting that happened to you. Tell three things you would do to make listeners feel that it is exciting.

Using the Glossary

Get to Know It!

The **Glossary** gives the meaning of a word as it is used in the story. It also gives an example sentence that shows how to use the word. A **synonym**, which is a word that has the same meaning, a **base word**, or **additional word forms** may come after the example sentence. The words in the **Glossary** are in ABC order, also called **alphabetical order**.

Learn to Use It!

If you want to find *cranes* in the **Glossary**, you should first find the *C* words. *C* is near the beginning of the alphabet, so the *C* words are near the beginning of the **Glossary**. Then you can use the guide words at the top of the page to help you find the entry word *cranes*. It is on page 452.

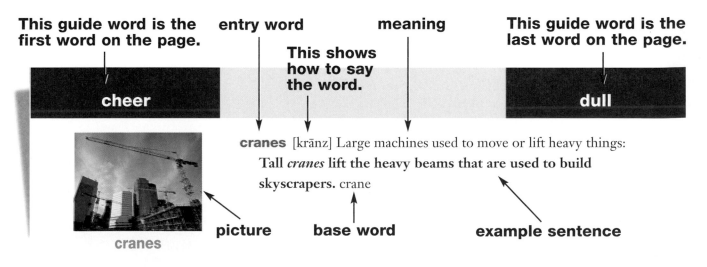

This guide word is the first word on the page.

entry word

meaning

This guide word is the last word on the page.

This shows how to say the word.

cheer

dull

cranes [krānz] Large machines used to move or lift heavy things: Tall *cranes* lift the heavy beams that are used to build skyscrapers. crane

picture

base word

example sentence

cranes

a·lone [ə·lōn′] Away from everyone else; by oneself: **Matt was *alone* in the yard after the other children went into the house.**

a·long·side [ə·lông′sīd′] Beside; at the side of: **Park your bike** *alongside* **the fence.**

al·ways [ôl′wāz *or* ôl′wēz] Every time: **He is *always* on time.**

a·maz·ing [ə·mā′zing] Surprising: **It is truly *amazing* how good Morgan is at socccer.** amaze, amazed

an·nounced [ə·nounst′] Told others some news or information: **Our teacher *announced* to the class that we would have a special visitor.** announce, announcing

ar·rived [ə·rīvd′] Got to a place: **His plane *arrived* at the airport on time.** arrive, arriving

bat·ter [bat′ər] A mixture of flour, milk, eggs, and other things that will be made into a cake or pancakes: **Pour the cake *batter* into the pan and bake it.**

beau·ti·ful [byoo′tə·fəl] Nice to look at: **The butterfly was so** *beautiful* **that I painted a picture of it.** *syns.* pretty, lovely

be·neath [bi·nēth′] Under: **We found the cat hiding *beneath* the sofa.**

boast·ed [bōst′əd] Talked in a bragging manner: **Ryan *boasted* that he was the best actor in the play.** boast, boasting

but·ter·y [but′ər·ē] Having butter on it: **My fingers are *buttery* from the toast I just ate.**

batter

beneath

451

chipmunks

cranes

cheer [chēr] To make someone who is unhappy feel better: **You can make a card to *cheer* a sick friend.** cheered, cheering

chip·munks [chip′mungks] Animals that look like small squirrels with stripes on their backs: **Two *chipmunks* ran under our porch.** chipmunk

chores [chôrz] Jobs that people do at home: **Setting the table and weeding the garden are two of my *chores*.** chore

clus·tered [klus′tərd] Got close together: **All the children *clustered* around the kitten.** cluster, clustering

cranes [krānz] Large machines used to move or lift heavy things: **Tall *cranes* lift the heavy beams that are used to build skyscrapers.** crane

crept [krept] Crawled: **We *crept* into the bushes when we played hide-and-seek.** creep, creeping

crown [kroun] An object worn on the head as a sign of honor: **Alice wore a silver *crown* as the princess in the play.**

di·rec·tions [di•rek′shənz] Plans that tell how to do something or how to go somewhere: **Read the game's *directions* so you will know what to do.** *syn.* instructions

dis·cov·er [dis•kuv′ər] To learn or find out: **What did you *discover* when you walked in the woods?** discovery

dull [dul] Not bright or shiny: **This bike was bright blue when it was new, but now its paint is *dull*.**

en·er·gy [en′ər·jē] A force that can give something power: **The *energy* of rushing water turns machines to make electricity.**

en·gine [en′jin] The part of a car or other machine that causes it to move: **Dad opened the hood of the car so we could see the *engine*.**

e·nor·mous [i·nôr′məs] Very, very big: **The fish was so *enormous* that it wouldn't fit in the boat!** *syn.* huge

ex·cit·ing [ik·sī′ting] Stirring up strong, lively feelings: **The movie was so *exciting* that we forgot to eat our popcorn.** *syn.* thrilling

engine

fine [fīn] Good: **We had a *fine* time at the fair.**

fore·cast [fôr′kast] To predict, or say ahead of time, what will happen: **I'd like to learn how to *forecast* the weather.** forecasting, forecaster

fron·tier [frun·tir′] A place where people have not lived before: **Years ago, people moved to the *frontier* to find new land for homes and farms.**

frontier

gath·ered [gath′ərd] Came together in a group: **The family *gathered* around Grandpa to listen to his story.** gather, gathering

glum [glum] Very unhappy: **Andy has been *glum* all day because his bike is missing.** *syns.* sad, gloomy

grand·daugh·ter [grand′dô•tər] The daughter of a person's son or daughter: **The grandparents took care of their little *granddaughter* while her parents worked.**

grew [grōō] Got bigger: **The little tree *grew* to be very tall.** grow, grown, growing

hand·some [han′səm] Good-looking: **A tiger has a *handsome* striped coat.**

hard·ly [härd′lē] Almost not: **He could *hardly* lift the heavy box.**

home·work [hōm′wûrk] Schoolwork done at home: **Our teacher gives us *homework* every night.**

knelt

knelt [nelt] Got down on one's knees: **He *knelt* down to pick up the pen he had dropped.** kneel, kneeling

meadow

mead·ow [med′ō] An open place where grass grows: **The cows ate grass in the *meadow*.**

mem·bers [mem′bərz] People who belong to a group such as a club or a team: **All the *members* of our reading group liked the story.** member

minutes [min′its] Sets of sixty seconds: **Dad told us to wait a few more *minutes* before leaving.** minute

454

near·by [nir·bī′] Not far; close by: **Mother stays *nearby* to watch us when we swim.**

nu·tri·tion [noo·trish′ən] Food for health and growth: **Children need *nutrition* to stay healthy.**

or·chards [ôr′chərdz] Large groups of fruit trees or nut trees that people have planted: **Some farmers have planted *orchards* of apple, pear, and other fruit trees.** orchard

orchard

per·fect [pûr′fikt] The best that something can be: **It was warm and sunny, a *perfect* day for a picnic.**

picked [pikt] Took something such as a flower, a fruit, or a vegetable from a plant: **She *picked* a big bunch of flowers from her garden.** pick, picking

plant·ed [plant′əd] Put something into the ground so it would grow: **These flowers grew from the seeds we *planted*.** plant, planting

prom·ise [prom′is] A statement that a person really will do something: **Don't make a *promise* if you are not sure you can keep it.**

pro·tects [prə·tekts′] Keeps safe: **Some animals have thick fur that *protects* them from the cold.** protect, protected, protecting

raced [rāst] Went very fast from one place to another: **Jenny** *raced* **home from school to tell her mother the good news.** race, racing

rea·son [rē′zən] A statement that tells why someone did something or why something happened: **The** *reason* **they are late is that the bus broke down.**

re·build [rē·bild′] To build again: **The farmer had to** *rebuild* **his barn after it burned down.** rebuilt, rebuilding

rec·i·pe [res′ə·pē] A plan that tells what items you need and what steps to follow to make something to eat or drink: **This** *recipe* **for popovers says to add two eggs.**

re·lay race [rē′lā rās] A race in which members of a team take turns running parts of the race: **In the** *relay race*, **each person on the team had to run to the tree and back.**

rip·ens [rī′pənz] Becomes fully grown or ready to be used as food: **A tomato turns from green to red as it** *ripens*. ripen, ripened, ripening

shed [shed] To throw off: **We kept dry because our plastic ponchos** *shed* **the rain.** sheds, shedding

shim·mered [shim′ərd] Shone with a soft sparkle: **The moonlight** *shimmered* **on the lake.** shimmer, shimmering

side·ways [sīd′wāz] To one side or the other: **I try to swim in a straight line, but I keep going** *sideways*.

recipe

relay race

456

sim·ple [sim′pəl] Easy to do or to understand: **Some math problems are hard, but this one is *simple*.**

smeared [smird] Spread something wet or greasy onto something else: **My little sister *smeared* finger paints all over the wall.** smear, smearing

sniff·ing [snif′ing] Breathing in through the nose in order to smell something: **Everyone kept *sniffing* the roses because they smelled so good.** sniff, sniffed

snug [snug] Warm and comfortable: **The children were *snug* in their warm beds that winter night.** *syn.* cozy

snug·gle [snug′əl] To hold close; cuddle: **I love to *snuggle* my baby sister in my arms.**

source [sôrs] A thing or person from which something comes: **Trees are a *source* of food and shelter for many animals.**

south [south] The direction to your right as you face the sunrise: **The plane turned and headed *south*.**

spar·kling [spär′kling] Shining in the light as a jewel does: **The dew on the grass was *sparkling* in the sunlight.** sparkle, sparkled *syn.* glittering

spoiled [spoild] Ruined; no longer useful: **The picture I drew was *spoiled* when I left it outside in the rain.** spoil, spoiling

spot·ted [spot′id] Saw something that might not be easy to see: **We *spotted* a plane flying high above.** spot, spotting

sprout [sprout] Begin to grow: **When the seeds *sprout*, tiny plants will push up through the ground.** sprouted, sprouting

streams [strēmz] Small rivers: **Fish live in ponds, lakes, rivers, *streams*, and oceans.** stream

strong [strông] Full of power; not weak: **The wind was so *strong* that it blew down some big trees.**

sniffing

sur·vive [sər·vīv′] To stay alive: **Desert plants and animals can** *survive* **without much water.** survived, surviving

tame [tām] To make something less wild: **You should not try to** *tame* **a wild animal by petting it.** tamed, taming

tool [tōōl] A thing you use to help you do work: **A drill is a** *tool* **that you can use to make holes in wood or metal.**

treat [trēt] Food or drink given or paid for by another: **Our coach bought each of us an ice cream** *treat* **after we won the game.**

tur·nip [tûr′nip] A round vegetable that grows under the ground and may be white or yellow: **Mother cooked the** *turnip* **so we could eat it with our dinner.**

twitch [twich] To move quickly a part of the face or body: **I like to watch rabbits** *twitch* **their noses.** twitched, twitching

vil·lage [vil′ij] A group of houses in the country: **We drove through a small** *village* **when we got off the main road.** *syn.* town

vines [vīnz] Plants with stems that grow along the ground or climb by clinging to something: **The** *vines* **twisted along my granddad's back fence.** vine

wan·dered [wän′dərd] Walked as people do when they are not in a hurry: **We looked at bugs and smelled the flowers as we** *wandered* **across the field.** wander, wandering

turnip

wild [wīld] Not lived on or used by people: **Our country has made parks where no one may build so that the land will stay** *wild*.

woods [woȯdz] A place where many trees grow: **Deer and other animals live in the** *woods*. *syn.* forest

wor·ry [wur′ē] To be upset by thinking about something that might happen: **When it doesn't rain, farmers** *worry* **that their crops will dry up.** worried, worrying

wrin·kled [ring′kəld] Became less smooth: **The clothes** *wrinkled* **in the hot dryer.** wrinkle, wrinkling

Y

yel·low cake [yel′ō kāk] A kind of cake that is yellow in color: **Would you like a** *yellow cake* **or a chocolate cake for your birthday?**

woods

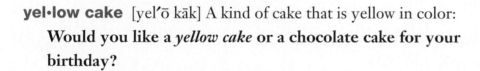

wrinkled

yellow cake

Index _of_ Titles

Page numbers in color tell where you can read about the author.

Acknowledgments

For permission to reprint copyrighted material, grateful acknowledgment is made to the following sources:

Bayard Presse Canada Inc., Toronto, Canada: From "Fun Animal Facts," illustrated by Steve Attoe in *Chickadee* Magazine, April 1997. © 1997 by Owl Communications Corp.

Candlewick Press Inc., Cambridge, MA, on behalf of Walker Books Ltd., London: Illustration from *Days Like This* by Simon James. Illustration © 1999 by Simon James.

Clarion Books/Houghton Mifflin Company: From *Helping Out* by George Ancona. Copyright © 1985 by George Ancona.

Dorling Kindersley Limited, London: From *The Secret Life of Trees* by Chiara Chevallier. Copyright © 1999 by Dorling Kindersley Limited, London.

Harcourt, Inc.: From *Mr. Putter and Tabby Fly the Plane* by Cynthia Rylant, illustrated by Arthur Howard. Text copyright © 1997 by Cynthia Rylant; illustrations copyright © 1997 by Arthur Howard.

HarperCollins Publishers: *The Mixed-Up Chameleon* by Eric Carle. Copyright © 1975, 1984 in countries signatory to International Copyright Union. From *Days With Frog and Toad* by Arnold Lobel. Copyright © 1979 by Arnold Lobel. *Get Up and Go!* by Stuart J. Murphy, illustrated by Diane Greenseid. Text copyright © 1996 by Stuart J. Murphy; illustrations copyright © 1996 by Diane Greenseid. *Lemonade for Sale* by Stuart J. Murphy, illustrated by Tricia Tusa. Text copyright © 1998 by Stuart J. Murphy; illustrations copyright © 1998 by Tricia Tusa. *Pumpkin Fiesta* by Caryn Yacowitz, illustrated by Joe Cepeda. Text copyright © 1998 by Caryn Yacowitz; illustrations copyright © 1998 by Joe Cepeda.

Holiday House, Inc.: From *Seed to Plant* by Gail Gibbons. Copyright © 1991 by Gail Gibbons.

Henry Holt and Company, LLC: *Watermelon Day* by Kathi Appelt, illustrated by Dale Gottlieb. Text copyright © 1996 by Kathi Appelt; illustrations copyright © 1996 by Dale Gottlieb.

Pyke Johnson, Jr.: "Lemonade" by Pyke Johnson, Jr.

Little, Brown and Company (Inc.): From *All Join In* by Quentin Blake. Copyright © 1990 by Quentin Blake. "Sometimes" from *Fathers, Mothers, Sisters, Brothers* by Mary Ann Hoberman, cover illustration by Marilyn Hafner. Text copyright © 1991 by Mary Ann Hoberman; illustration copyright © 1991 by Marilyn Hafner.

National Wildlife Federation: "Leaf Zoo" from *Your Big Backyard* Magazine, November, 1999. Text copyright © 1999 by National Wildlife Federation.

Random House Children's Books, a division of Random House, Inc., New York, NY: *Hedgehog Bakes a Cake* by Maryann Macdonald, illustrated by Lynn Munsinger. Copyright © 1990 by Byron Preiss Visual Publications, Inc. Text copyright © 1990 by Maryann Macdonald; illustrations copyright © 1990 by Lynn Munsinger.

Marian Reiner, on behalf of Aileen Fisher: "The Seed" from *Up the Windy Hill* by Aileen Fisher. Text copyright © 1953 by Aileen Fisher; text © renewed 1981 by Aileen Fisher.

Simon & Schuster Books for Young Readers, an imprint of Simon & Schuster Children's Publishing Division: *Wilson Sat Alone* by Debra Hess, illustrated by Diane Greenseid. Text copyright © 1994 by Debra Hess; illustrations copyright © 1994 by Diane Greenseid. From *Henry and Mudge Under the Yellow Moon* by Cynthia Rylant, illustrated by Suçie Stevenson. Text copyright © 1987 by Cynthia Rylant; illustrations copyright © 1987 by Suçie Stevenson.

Walker and Company: Illustrations from *Look What I Did With a Leaf* by Morteza Sohi. Illustrations copyright © by Morteza Sohi.

Photo Credits

Key: (t)=top; (b)=bottom; (c)=center; (l)=left; (r)=right
Page 14(t), Leonard L.T. Rhodes / Earth Scenes; 14(b), Jeanne White / Photo Researchers, Inc.; 15(t), Stan Osolinski / Dembinsky Photo Associates; 15(b),Tom Brakefield / Corbis Stock Market; 47, courtesy, Eric Carle; 77(bl), Jim Coit / Black Star; 77(br), Larry Evans / Black Star; 94(bl), Carlo Ontal; 95(br), Rick Friedman / Black Star; 117(br), courtesy, HarperCollins; 121(b), Culver Pictures; 145(bl), 145(br), Black Star; 169(bl), Archive Photos; 174-186, George Ancona; 187, Helga Ancona; 191(bl), Free Library of Philadelphia; 218(tl), Carlo Ontal; 219(br), Dale Higgins; 220(br), 221(tr), 223(tr), Harcourt; 246®, David Levenson / Black Star; 247(l), Walt Chrynwski / Black Star; 249(all), Harcourt; 251(b), Superstock; 275(bl), Larry Evans / Black Star; 275(br), Black Star; 305(bl), Dominic Oldershaw; 305(br), Black Star; 312(tr), Harcourt Photo Library; 312©, Mark Turner; 312(bl), Thompson & Thompson / Stone; 313(all), Harcourt Photo Library; 331, courtesy, Gail Gibbons; 334(br), 335(tr), Harcourt Photo Library; 336, Photodisc.com; 340-341, 342(tl), (tr), (cl), DK Publishing; 342(br), Bruce Coleman Collection; 343, DK Publishing; 344(br), Empics; 344, DK Publishing; 345(t), Dr. Eckart Pott / Bruce Coleman Collection; 345(br), John Shaw / Bruce Coleman Collection; 345©, DK Publishing; 346(all), Bruce Coleman Collection; 347-348, DK Publishing; 349(tr), DK Publishing; 349(seasons), Pictor International Ltd.; 349(br), DK Publishing; 350(tr), Telegraph Colour Library; 350(bl), Sir Jeremy Grayson / Bruce Coleman Collection; 350(cb), 351, DK Publishing; 352(tr), Dorling Kindersley Picture Library/Natural History Museum; 352©, Mark Taylor / Bruce Coleman Collection; 353, 354, 355, DK Publishing; 358(ct), DK Publishing; 358(bl), Pictor International Ltd.; 359(ct), DK Publishing; 389(bl), courtesy, Kathi Appelt; 389(br), Black Star; 391(cr), (br), Harcourt Photo Library; 420(cb), Dale Higgins; 421(cb), Peter Stone / Black Star; 432(cb), Harcourt Photo Library; 450, G. Ryan & S. Beyer / Stone; 452(t), Tom McHugh / Photo Researchers, Inc.; 452(b), G. Ryan & S. Beyer / Stone; 453(t), Paul Chauncey / Corbis Stock Market; 453(b), Harcourt Photo Library; 454(t), Ken Kinzie / Harcourt; 454(b), Oddo Sinibaldi / Corbis Stock Market; 455, Dick Thomas / Visuals Unlimited; 458, Ken Kinzie / Harcourt; 459(t), Terry Donnelly / Tom Stack & Associates; 459©, Ken Kinzie / Harcourt; 459(b), Harcourt Photo Library.

Illustration Credits

Scott Gustafson, Cover Art; Tom Casmer, 4-5, 12-13; Jennie Oppenheimer, 6-7, 150-151; Donna Perrone, 8-9, 282-283; Ethan Long 10-11, 51, 220-221; Eric Carle, 16-47; Jackie Snider, 52, 97; Tracy Sabin, 54-55; Diane Greenseid, 56-77, 126-145; Cathy Bennet, 79, 80, 147, 168-169,170, 222-223, 422-423; Melissa Iwai, 82-83; Suçie Stevenson, 84-95; Nancy Coffelt 98, 250-251, 424; Robert Casilla, 100-101; Arnold Lobel, 102-117; Steve Johnson/Lou Fancher, 118-119; Nancy Davis, 120-121, 224; Betsy Everitt, 124-125; Chris Van Dusen, 146-147, 252; Mike Tofanelli, 152-153; Scott Gotto, 154-167; Tim Bowers, 172-173; Laura Ovresat, 190-191, 364-365; Fabricio Vanden Broeck, 194-195; Arthur Howard, 196-219; Tiphanie Beeke, 226-227; Lynn Munsinger, 228-247; Melinda Levine, 254-255; Tricia Tusa, 256-275; Jennifer Beck-Harris, 276-277; Sudi McCullum, 284-285; Victoria Raymond, 286-305, 310-311; Gail Gibbons, 314-331; Dale Verzaal, 336-337; Marla Baggetta, 338-339; Tuko Fujisaki, 362-363; Rebecca Gibbon, 366-367; Dale Gottlieb, 368-389; Jon Berkeley, 394-395; Joe Cepeda, 396-421; Holly Cooper 451, 457.

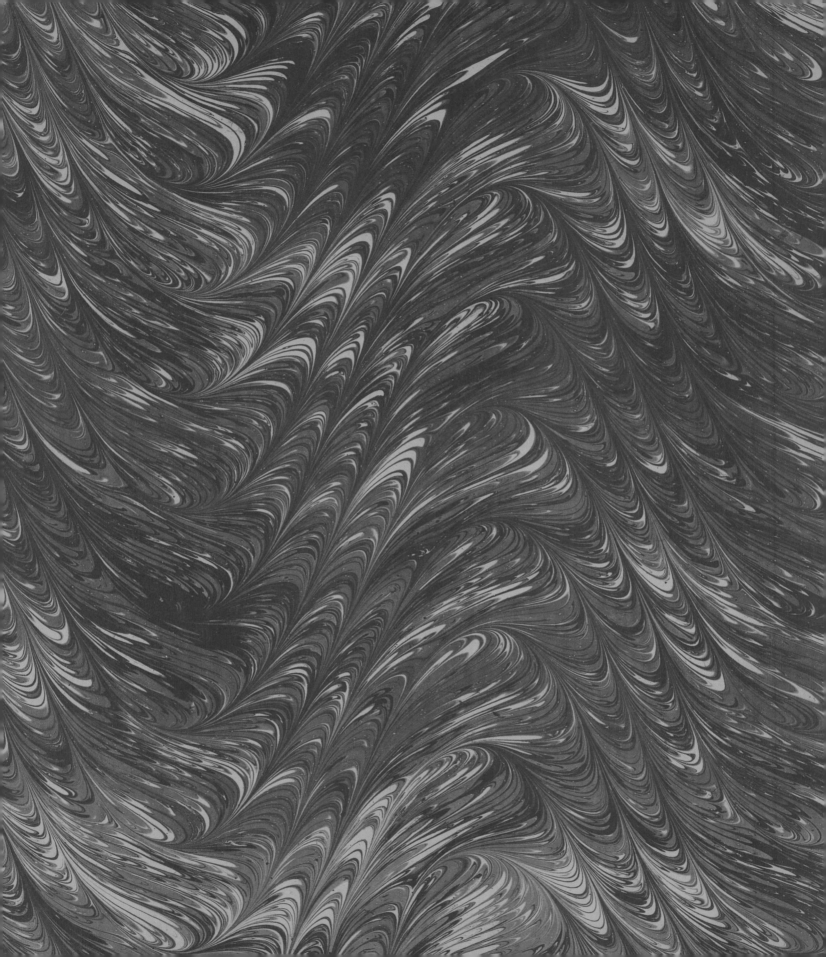